EKKLESIA DECLARED!

Becoming Who You Were Designed to Be

Julie —
May God come to
have First Place in
everything.
Rolland
Col. 1:18b

By Rolland Wright

Published by

Wright Publishing Company
3616 Colby Ave. #788, Everett, WA 98201
Phone: 844-494-3697
Website: www.firstplaceministries.com
Email: Rolland@firstplaceministries.com

Copyright Use and Public Information

Unless otherwise noted, images have been used according to public information laws.

ISBN: **ISBN: 978-0-578-33901-6** Paperback

Limits of Liability and Disclaimer of Warranty The author and publisher shall not be liable for the reader's misuse of this material. This book is for strictly informational and educational purposes.

Scriptures taken from the Tree of Life version © 2015 by the Messianic Jewish Family Bible Society. Used by permission of the Messianic Jewish Family Bible Society. "TLV" and "Tree of Life Version" and "Tree of Life Holy Scriptures" are trademarks registered in the United States Patent and Trademark office by the Messianic Family Bible Society.

Disclaimer

The views expressed are those of the author and do not reflect the official policy or position of the publisher or The Widows Project This publication is designed to provide accurate and authoritative information regarding the subject matter covered. It is sold with the understanding that the publisher is not engaged in rendering legal, accounting, clinical or other professional advice. If legal advice or other expert assistance is required, the services of a competent professional should be sought. The opinions expressed by the authors in this book are not endorsed by The Widows Project, and are the sole responsibility of the author rendering the opinion.

PRAISE FOR "EKKLESIA DECLARED!"

"My hunger for the Lord compels me to want to be on time and in season with His purposes in the earth and if you do too, you must read this book. Mr. Wright's revelation on where the Bod of Christ (Ekklesia) is and where we are in history as humanity is very, very eye opening and encouraging. I highly recommend it. The revelation in this book is critical for us as we enter this new season."

~ **Sharon Best** – Wife, Mom, Grandmother (Ammy), Certified Life Coach, Certified Restoring The Foundations Minister, Facilitator of Ekklesia War Room

"I am so grateful for Rolland and his efforts in this book, but more importantly in his life. We can no longer afford to give our time to those who communicate in words but lack the ability or willingness to do the works of Him who sent us. Status quo is now doing great harm to our families, our communities, our churches, and our nation. It is time to jettison the institutional baggage that has deceived us and return to the way God intends relational engagement. As one who has served in the military, started non-profits, planted churches, and now starting a school I can say God's way works and my way does not. A biblical model has always worked and will continue to be the one thing that works, and Rolland helps us see this and do this. It is simple, but it will not be easy. Yet the next generation depends on us getting back to God's way."

~ **Shawn O.Schrader**

ACKNOWLEDGMENTS

I want to recognize Dean Briggs and Tim Kurtz for their books, which served to bring me awareness and resolve over my confusion regarding church and my identity in Christ. I credit you both for the courage to stand in the face of the enemy and declare the truth.

Thank you ekklesia family, Arthur and Sharon Best, Jim and Jackie Morey. You have encouraged me and held me up in contending intercessory prayer for the duration. Our gatherings have modeled fellowship, genuine love and care for one another, worship, teaching, and communion.

I am thankful for the Familia De Oracao contending prayer group who have taught me the skills of fervent, passionate, urgent, disciplined prayer in the spirit. Thank you for allowing me to join you daily for the past six months. Our association has taken my prayer engagement to another level.

Thank you, Steve Anderson, for the hours of conversation about guidelines for meeting and establishing a model of what ekklesia could look like.

Jackie, your personal investment and skill do not go unnoticed. Thank you for your publishing and promotion skills.

Dedicated to those who have felt disenfranchised from the church and those who discover they have been deceived. You have a new identity and a new opportunity to become who Jesus declared you to be. Go and become the Ekklesia!

TABLE OF CONTENTS

INTRODUCTION

It is an amazing honor and daunting task when you know you have been given a purpose to fulfill. I come to you with hesitancy and reluctance mixed with a great measure of obedience. The content within is the product of a lifetime of process and Holy Spirit-prompting over the past two years.

In the past decade, I have been honored to found and establish *The Widows Project* as the premier grief support organization unique to widowhood. Its seven-year history is filled with challenges, none greater than the challenge of awakening the institutional church to the needs and care of the widowed.

Simultaneously, the Holy Spirit has tasked me with revealing and exposing the deception around the formation of the church as an institution. There has been confusion in the kingdom of God about the church. Is it people or is it a building? Is it a building or is it an institution? I have heard many sermons on Matthew 16:18 and never have I heard what I am about to reveal in this book.

If the church is people, like you and I, then why do we use the term church on our signage and buildings? Have you ever heard someone say, "I went to church today?" Or have you ever been asked, "Where do you go to church?" If you were to interview a person on the street, point to a building that looks like a place of

1

worship, and ask them, "What is that building called?", would they answer, "A church."? This proves that we have been doing a good job at indoctrinating the congregant and the non-congregant what we believe the church to be.

We have created an oxymoron, an untruth of our identity. We have perpetuated a lie and we have done it, repeated it, for centuries without challenge, all because a group of theologians acquiesced to a king's demands.

Since then, the community of faith has battled over the pre-tribulation/mid-tribulation and post-tribulation doctrine, sprouted denominational divisions, started cults, developed translations from translations (declared to be the most accurate translations), battled over denominational supremacy, and westernized theological concepts and constructs. I contend that God is sickened, repulsed by the implosion of the faith community.

There are similarities in today's global chaos, depravity, and oppression to that of the early community of faith's oppression at the hands of the Roman government. I hear and declare the word "Hoshia-na" (save now!) being the heart cry of the community of the ekklesia. The time is now for the "ekklesia" to rise up out of the ashes and engage in the new movement—a scriptural movement of God.

We desperately need to declare which God we are crying out to. For too long, we assumed that followers and non-followers of Jesus alike know to whom we are praying and of whom we are testifying. Let's leave no doubt. We believe, I believe, in the Hebrew God by all His names.

Here are links to videos on the wonderful Names of God:

Names of Jesus The Great I AM "365 Names" –
https://youtu.be/oEg7h4E2b7E

He is (The Names of God) – (Return of Majesty Trilogy) by
Eric Ludy – https://youtu.be/NscHCa395-M

Each name declares a characteristic of God that is immutable, unchanging, and steadfast. God made it extremely clear in the Torah that He is to be the only God, and we declare and confirm that there is no other. He wants; He demands exclusivity. He also wants undivided, total love with all (the entirety) our hearts, minds, and soul.

Do we think it is a new thing that "faith" and "government" are at odds with each other? One must only read the book of Esther to find an early example of a decree given by a king to exterminate the Jewish people. Or, consider the book of Daniel when he and his three exiled Hebrew friends were required, like the rest of the nation, to bow down to a "golden image" or face death by fire.

They collectively chose to defy the king's orders and were thrown into the fire. One only needs to read the Gospel to understand the oppression of the Jewish nation at the hand of Roman soldiers. It was the Roman government that did the bidding of the religious Pharisees and arrested Jesus and hung him on a cross. Post-resurrection, the early faith community — followers of Jesus — were summarily suppressed, which led to the "diaspora" and a great movement of the Holy Spirit and the spreading of the gospel.

If you are not aware, the gospel was so threatening to the government of man that the apostles, except John, were martyrs for the Messiah.

The suppression of the gospel, and the community of faith I choose to call the Ekklesia, is not a new phenomenon. World powers have been using the tool of suppression for centuries. Here is a brief historical overview for the past 500 years.

When Martin Luther penned and nailed his 95 Theses to the doors of Wittenburg Castle, he served notice to the Catholic Church in protest (Protestant movement). The year was 1517, October 31st, five hundred years ago. The three main points of the Theses are:

(1) Selling indulgences to finance the building of St. Peter's is wrong.

(2) The pope has no power over Purgatory.

(3) Buying indulgences gives people a false sense of security and endangers their salvation.

(From A Summary of the Ninety-Five Theses secured from an article by Uncommon Travel Germany, no date or author cited, The 95 Theses: A Summary (uncommon-travel-germany.com)

The nerve of a man like Martin Luther to stand up and defy the institution of Catholicism and the Pope. "It should be noted that it was in the century following Martin Luther that King James authorized the switch from ekklesia to church." (Tim Kurtz, pg. 147, Leaving Church/Becoming Ekklesia).

Then along came a man named William Tyndale who is credited with printing the first English Bible translated from the original Greek and Hebrew. Why all the uproar over an English Bible translation? Former translations in English were taken from the Latin Vulgate, the Catholic translation. Thus, they (the Vatican) assumed universal authority over the scriptures and controlled the narrative in Latin. Any attempt to translate to English was seen as a huge threat and deemed illegal.

Let's retrace history. More than a thousand years before Tyndale, Saint Jerome translated the Bible into Latin and produced what became known as the Vulgate. Being in Latin, it was recognized as the word of God and became the Catholic Bible. Along came another scholar by the name of John Wycliffe who took the Vulgate and translated word for word into English. Then he began criticizing the clergy's theology and practices.

So, when Tyndale came along, the Catholic Church had seen this kind of trouble before and they didn't like it. Tyndale's translation undercut the control of the Catholic Church. Tyndale's defiance of the earthly religious powers that be led to his death. In fact, 40 years after his death, they dug up his body, burned it, and threw the ashes in the river.

Over the next few years, Tyndale wrote, continued translating the Old Testament, and improved his translations of the New Testament. During this time, he befriended a man named Henry Phillips, who had recently gambled away a bunch of his father's money. Henry was one of the only people Tyndale allowed to see his writings.

In 1535, Henry betrayed Tyndale and handed him over to Belgian soldiers, who threw him in prison and charged him with heresy.

After a months-long process, the church stripped Tyndale of his priesthood, condemned him as a heretic, and passed him to the state.

Then they tied him to a stake, strangled him to death with a noose, and burned him alive dead.

Tyndale – betrayed by a friend, condemned by the church, and executed by the state.

In his *Book of Martyrs*, John Foxe reports that Tyndale's last words were: "Lord! Open the King of England's eyes." (From the article: Who Was William Tyndale? By Ryan Nelson, October 5, 2018). Interesting highlight: In this same article, he claims that Tyndale was the first to produce an English translation of the Bible from the original Greek and Hebrew. Mr. Tyndale was fluent in eight languages.

Mr. Nelson also claims that Tyndale was called a "Lollard" — a derogatory term for uneducated people. Wycliffe was an educated Seminary Professor at the University of Oxford until he started going after the clergy.

"By what authority did the Lollards dare to defy the Catholic Church? The Bible!"

And how could these uneducated people claim to know what God's Word said about any of these (spiritual) things? "Because Wycliffe put the English Bible in their hands."

I know I don't possess a list of titles and degrees behind my name, but I know I have the same, One and only Holy Spirit, who, like Peter in Matthew 16: 17, led Jesus to declare, "flesh and blood did not reveal this to you, but My Father in heaven".

A hundred years later, another man makes a bold assertion and declares himself as the head of the Church of England. He finances a new translation of the Bible (which ironically is _mostly_ based on Tyndale's translation) and names it after himself. *The word "mostly" is important, as the king did require some key changes to the translation, which we will discuss later.*

So, I invite you to join me on a journey. A journey to discover what Jesus declared. He gave us lots of "CLUES" in the Bible. Let's investigate together and follow the "CLUES" and see if we will end up with the same conclusions. It is of uttermost importance if we want to be obedient and who He declared us to be.

CHAPTER 1

ARE YOU ABLE TO LOOK BEYOND THE TREES?

"He can't see the forest for the trees." An old English expression was already a proverb in John Heywood's 1546 collection. The general sense is that someone is missing the bigger picture because they are too focused on the smaller details.

CLUE: SQUIRREL! Don't get so easily distracted and miss the BIG PICTURE!

There is a saying I have not heard for years, which says, "He can't see the forest for the trees." What does this statement mean? It means we can get so tunnel-visioned that we do not see what is going on around us. It is our inability to understand or focus on a situation in its entirety because we are preoccupied with minor details. This means that if we only focus on what is immediately in front of us, we are distracted from seeing what is happening beyond our vision. We are facing this dynamic in our world today.

It is easy to see our bank accounts dwindling, to see subtle shifts of emptying shelves at our supermarkets, weather shifts to support changes in our climates, mandates requiring us to choose life over careers, but if we don't stand back and away from what is directly in front of us, we miss the bigger picture.

We face this dynamic in our physical and our spiritual lives. I encourage you to take a few cleansing breaths, lower your heart rate, and stand back and even elevate your ability to see over and beyond the trees of life. I hope to establish that there is a bigger picture and a bigger battle going on in our world today, and we are being distracted from seeing it. Our ability or inability to get beyond the distractions will proportionally impact our comprehension of what is happening.

What is happening to us directly is a microcosm of what is happening in our states, our nations, and globally. Fortunately, with the help of the internet, we are infinitely more aware than the previous generations when it comes to what is happening beyond our vision. Yet, much is being hidden purposefully from us. The disinformation and lies have always been prominent, but they have been taken to a new level with social media with the aid of the master schemer. The sheer level of evil and corruption surpasses the era of Noah, Sodom, and Gomorrah. We are at war and approaching either a course correction, a reconciliation, a reckoning, or Christ's return. I encourage you to join me on a journey of discovery. We are going to accomplish this primarily from the Word of God, the Bible. Why? Because He wrote it for our instruction and as our primary source for answers.

I am going to utilize a board game I played as an adolescent, called "CLUE!", a murder mystery, who done it game. My generation will understand, but for those who are younger and have not played the game, here are the basic rules and guidelines of the game. CLUE utilized a game board that portrayed the interior blueprint of a mansion and its various rooms. Cards were provided in three categories: the characters or suspects, the weapons of choice, and the possible rooms of the mansion in which the crime was committed. Each category of cards was shuffled and one card from each category was placed in a secret envelope, which was not revealed until someone made a guess as to who committed the murder, with what weapon, and in which room. The winner was the first to solve all three accusations.

We may as well begin at the alpha point, the beginning as recorded by Moses in the book of Genesis, the beginnings.

CLUE: Obtain new "CLUE(S)" in each chapter!

CHAPTER 2

GENESIS: WHERE IT ALL BEGAN, WHEN IT ALL BEGAN, HOW IT ALL BEGAN, AND WHO ARE THE CHARACTERS INVOLVED IN THE GREATEST STORY EVER TOLD

"I had noticed, of course, that the humans were having a lull in their European war — what they naively call 'The War'! -- and am not surprised that there is a corresponding lull in the patient's anxieties. Do we want to encourage this, or to keep him worried? Tortured fear and stupid confidence are both desirable states of mind. Our choice between them raises important questions." ~C.S. Lewis, The Screwtape Letters

"But the serpent was shrewder than any animal of the field that ADONAI Elohim made. So it said to the woman, "Did God really say, 'You must not eat from all the trees of the garden'? The woman said to the serpent, "Of the fruit of the trees, we may eat. But of the fruit of the tree, which is in the middle of the garden, God said, 'You must not eat of it and you must not touch it, or you will die.'" The serpent said to the woman, "You most assuredly won't die! For God knows that when you eat of it, your eyes will be opened and you will be like God, knowing good and evil." Now the woman saw that the tree was good for food, and that it was a thing of lust for the eyes, and that the tree

was desirable for imparting wisdom. So she took of its fruit and she ate. She also gave her husband who was with her and he ate. Then the eyes of both of them were opened and they knew that they were naked; so they sewed fig leaves together and made for themselves loin-coverings. And they heard the sound of ADONAI Elohim going to and fro in the garden in the wind of the day. So the man and his wife hid from the presence of ADONAI Elohim in the midst of the Tree of the garden." Genesis 3:1-8 God, man, woman, serpent.

From the beginning of Genesis, we are introduced to God first! He gives no argument for His existence but an announcement that He is. A synopsis of His creative days are given to us sequentially and include the creation of man. We are told that God, within all of his creative process, did not find a "well-matched helper" for the first man, Adam. So, "Adonai Elohim caused a deep sleep to fall on the man and he slept; and He took one of his ribs and closed up the flesh in its place. Adonai Elohim built the rib, which He had taken from the man, into a woman."

By Genesis Chapter 3, we are introduced to a fourth entity important to understanding everyone involved in the narrative of this text and active in the world, both physical and spiritual. In time and space, both God and Satan are involved in man's life with influence, which has eternal consequences.

> *CLUE: According to the Genesis account, who is actively involved with man & woman, and influencing our lives for good or evil?*

If we recognize the Bible as the Word of God — infallible and accurate — we must recognize that from the very beginning God is announcing to us His involvement in the creation of the world and us, mankind and that there is an archrival, a villain, who is also actively involved in destroying what God has created.

If we see and acknowledge that this dynamic exists between God and man, and that there is an enemy opposed to God and man, then we need to carry this dynamic forward in space and time. This would include recognition of this dynamic in history and today.

If we can agree on this premise, we are a step closer to understanding what is happening in our world today. We need to step back and see above and beyond the visual of our immediate emotions and events of our personal lives and then compare that to the bigger picture of global forces that are shaping our nations, policies, international politics, governments, institutions, religion, medicine, communication, and education.

We must get beyond party identification, denominational affiliation, or being a patriot and recognize the corruption on both sides of the aisle. The satanic forces do not care about either party, any denomination, any club, fraternity, or patriotism. The only loyalty comes down to who you will serve!

If you are not convinced, not sure about Satan's existence, or involvement in the world, you need to read more of the bible. Moving forward in history, re-read the accounts of Jesus' first encounter after His baptism (Luke 4:1-13), or His power over

15

demons (Mark 5:1-20), or His encounter with "two demon-plagued men" (Matthew 8:28-34), or the account of Judah's betrayal of Jesus (Luke 22: 3). We need to also include the writings of Luke's account of the apostles casting out demons (Acts 16:16-18), or the experience of those who tried to impersonate the apostles (Acts 19:11-20).

We need to include Paul's writings about the forces we are fighting. It was in the past two years that I have come to appreciate and understand Ephesians 6:10-18, the passage we often recite but do not apply in the way we should.

> *"For our struggle is not against flesh and blood, but against the rulers, against the power, against the worldly forces of wickedness in the heavenly places."*

Do we take this passage to heart? Do we suit up in military gear every day ready for battle? There used to be a commercial for a credit card years ago, in which the tag line was, "Don't leave home without it!" I encourage you today to do no less. Do not venture out into the world without the armor of God!

We must know who the enemy is or else, how do we know who we are fighting? God gave us the answer in Genesis 3 and the following scriptures I have highlighted. There are more scriptures I could have listed, but you have enough to establish that we have a real enemy, and he seeks to kill, steal, destroy, and do much more harm to us than we realize. Many of us are naively underestimating our true enemy. Can we agree that God has warned us repeatedly?

Also, be assured that your enemy is fighting against you, whether or not you want to engage in fighting him back. If you don't have the armor of God, you are defenseless. You must begin with salvation. If you are not born again, you have no armor. Salvation is the key piece of the armor; the first piece. Know that you are born again. Then, allow the Holy Spirit to armor you up piece by piece, by peace.

CHAPTER 3

HOW DID THE WHOLE IDEA OF
A KING COME ABOUT IN ISRAEL?

"We always have a role in our development. Gifts are free, maturity is expensive." Bill Johnson pg. 72 "Hosting the Presence"

Now when Samuel grew old, he appointed his sons as judges over Israel. The name of his firstborn was Joel and the name of his second Abijah — they were judges in Beersheba. His sons, however, did not walk in his ways, but turned aside after dishonest gain — they took bribes and perverted justice. 1 Samuel 8:1-3

"Now when these signs happen to you, do for yourself what the occasion requires, for God is with you." 1 Samuel 10:7

First a Theocracy

B efore there ever was a king, God ruled directly. He walked and talked with Adam. But in Genesis 12:1-3, we see these words spoken to Abram:

"Then ADONAI said to Abram, "Get going out from your land, and from your relatives, and from your father's house, to the land that I will show you. My heart's desire is to make you into a great nation, to bless you, to make your name great so that you may be a blessing. My desire is to bless those who bless you, but whoever curses you I will curse, and in you all the families of the earth will be blessed."

God's plan to establish a national theocracy with His covenant people was revealed. Years later, after a four-hundred-year experience in Egypt, which ended in slavery, God heard the cries of His people and extracted them from the tyranny of Pharaoh through a man named Moses.

God gave Moses a staff and mouthpiece (Aaron) and systematically eliminated every false god of the Egyptians. The decimation of Egypt and her gods was so thorough that by the time the last plague hit, Pharaoh and his people were giving the Hebrew people whatever they wanted so they could just leave.

But like most kings, Pharaoh could not resist the temptation to go after Moses and the Hebrew nation for one last attempt to inflict some pain. Vindication came at a high price, however, because he was not dealing with Moses; he was facing off with the Living, Holy, Sovereign, Yahweh, The King of Kings. Moses was just the instrument; Yahweh was the force. It cost Pharaoh and his troops their lives. They had defied the Living God and paid dearly.

Then Moses climbs Mt. Sinai (several times) and meets with Elohim. He must have been in great physical health to carry stone tablets up and down a mountain as an old man. Here is what the Holman Illustrated Bible Dictionary says about "the giving of the Mosaic law by God to the Israelites, which gave the Hebrew people a unique theocratic structure. The civil and moral laws provided the guidance for the governance of the state and personal relationships within the theocracy. These laws would establish the basic social structures of the theocratic state: judicial decision-making, processes of adjudication, marital guidelines, parental responsibilities, regard for human life, property rights, and so forth. The ceremonial law addressed the issues of religious observances and practice (pg. 1580)."

God Directs and Orders

> *Clue: Does the Garden of Eden*
> *Link to the Tabernacle?*

[https://bibleproject.com/explore/video/priests-of-eden/?utm_source=web_social_share&medium=shared_video]

While in the desert, God also gave them all the details, plans, and instructions for the making of the Tabernacle and all its furnishings, implements, and elements. He even plats the order, positioning, and layout of the entire camp with the Tabernacle in the center. He designates and appoints the tribe of Levi as the priestly order. Not all Levites were priests, but all priests came from this tribe. They are instructed on all the tasks of being priests and High Priest. How is the Ark of the Covenant to be

21

handled and carried? God was precise in all the details of His dwelling place and His presence.

During this forty-year wilderness experience, God shows Himself — His presence — as a "cloud by day and a pillar of fire at night." If you have ever spent any time in a desert environment, you know how hot temperatures can climb during the day. And at night, temperatures can dive to freezing. Without a covering during the day and a heat source at night, the Hebrew nation could not have survived. God not only provided miracle food and water, but He also provided comfort and protection from the elements. He was physically and spiritually with them.

There are times I look at all the things God did for this nation and yet, while Moses was on the mountain, they surrounded Aaron and begged him to "make us gods who will go before us (Exodus 32:1b)." How could they trade inanimate objects, which could not breathe, for the hand and the presence of the living God? And yet, we act out similarly. We have our idols and objects of affection. I will give you one example from my life.

Our nation has an addiction to sports. I used to love playing sports and watching them. This addiction requires a lot of one's time, especially if you want to excel. All the hours of practice and preparation. All the travel and expenses of the best gear available. All the discipline and off-field training if you are an athlete. If you are also a fan, the investment in time (average professional or college game is 3 hrs.), gear of your favorite team or teams, tickets, and parking costs. For many, it is a religion and even for the follower of Jesus, sports became an obsession.

For all the years the Super Bowl has been in existence, Churches used to change service times or cancel services that conflicted with the event. People even wear their gear to Church. Is it possible that God has felt displaced or forsaken? All I can say is that, over the past couple of years, sports have plummeted on my list of priorities. I have repented of my indulgences of time watching sports and worshipping at the throne of college and professional sports. If you cannot honestly say that God has first place in your heart (Col. 1:18b) and an exclusive relationship (no other gods or idols) with you, then I encourage you to put everything in place by forsaking it and reconciling with God. He is eternal. Everything else is temporary. This world is not our home. James 4:4 captures it all:

> *"You adulteresses! Don't you know that friendship with the world is enmity with God? Therefore, whoever wishes to be a friend of the world makes himself an enemy of God."*

God calls it "adultery;" that is, to run off with another god. He, like your wife, likes exclusivity. He doesn't want part of you or a portion of your heart. He wants all of you.

For all followers of Jesus, look at it this way. Jesus is called the bridegroom for a reason. We are called His bride. He is jealous for you. Quit lusting and flirting with the world. We run off with our desires and lusts and wonder why God would struggle with that.

There are two verses found in 1 Corinthians 10: 6 & 11 that are almost identical. Paul tells us, *"Now these things happened as examples for us so we wouldn't crave evil things just as they did." "Now these things happened to them as an example, and it was written down as a warning to us."*

Allow me to give a Wright's paraphrase: "The Bible is complete with instruction about everything under the sun. These examples of people who sinned and did not follow my instructions are written down so that you won't have to experience the pain and suffering they did." Biblical instruction is to no avail if we don't read it, heed it, and obey it.

I just gave sports as an example because it was an area I struggled with for years. When I was young, if there was a game on television (especially if they were my favorite teams) that I wanted to watch, I was in agony during church services. I could not wait to get home.

A Long Journey Home:
CLUE: ARE WE BETTER SERVED TO DO LIFE GOD'S WAY?

Let's journey with the Hebrew nation and move on into the Promised Land. God continues the Theocratic system He has established with Israel. Through the leadership of Joshua (Yahweh delivered), Yahweh brings them into the land. Through a series of fourteen battles (Joshua was 1-14), they take control of the land. There is much that could be discussed. But for the purposes of this conversation, I want to move to the apportionment of land.

Several years ago, I made some observations about the Twelve Tribes of Israel. First, let us establish for those who are not familiar with the Bible that the Twelve Tribes are twelve sons, and Israel is the name of their father as well as the name of a nation. As God did with other men at transitional times (Abram became Abraham and Saul became Paul), his name changed. In Genesis 35:9–12, we read this exchange:

> *God appeared to Jacob again after he returned from Paddan-aram, and He blessed him. God said to him: "Your name was Jacob. No longer will your name be Jacob, for your name will be Israel." So He named him Israel. God also said to him: "I am El Shaddai. Be fruitful and multiply. A nation and an assembly of nations will come from you. From your loins will come forth kings. The land that I gave to Abraham and to Isaac— I give it to you, and to your seed after you I will give the land."*

We hear sermons in which the Twelve Tribes are mentioned and throughout the Bible, the names change. They are not always consistently the same. Why? My chart tracks each boy/tribe in order of birth (Gen. 29-35), blessing (Gen. 49), land allotment (Josh.15-22:1-9), "by lot" (Ezekiel 48), and the "144,000" (Rev. 7).

Here is a chart I developed to help us make some interesting observations about why we see some names and not others.

THE TWELVE SONS OF JACOB (ISRAEL)

SON (BIRTH ORDER)	MOTHER	BLESSING (GEN. 49)	APPORTION (BY LOT) (JOSH. 15-22)	EZEKIEL 48 (BY LOT)	REVELATION 7 (144K)
01 Reuben Gen.29:32 "Behold a son"	Leah	1	5A (east of Jordan)	6	2
02 Simeon Gen. 29:33 "hearing"	Leah	2	7	10	7
03 Levi Gen. 29:34 "joined"	Leah	3	no land	8	8
04 Judah Gen. 29:35 "Let God be praised"	Leah	4	1	7	1
05 Dan Gen. 30:6 "judge"	Bilhah	7	12	1	missing
06 Napthtali Gen. 30:8 "my wrestling"	Bilhah	10	11	3	5
07 Gad Gen. 30:11 "good fortune"	Zilpah	8	5B (east of Jordan)	13	3
08 Asher Gen. 30:13 "happy"	Zilpah	9	10	2	4
09 Issachar Gen. 30:18 "man of hire"	Leah	6	9	11	9
10 Zebulun Gen. 30:20 "dwelling"	Dinah	5	8	12	10
11 Joseph Gen. 30:22-24 "may Jehovah add"	Rachel	11	#2 Ephraim & #3 Manasseh	4 Gen. 48 / Gen. 49 ½ 5C	J11/M6/E-MIA
12 Benjamin Gen. 35:18 "son of my sorrow"	Rachel	12	6	9	12

The first observation is that Israel had two wives (Leah & Rachel), and they each had handmaidens (Zilpah & Dinah, & Bilhah, respectively). To compound the situation, Leah and Rachel were sisters. It is an interesting story of how that transpired (Gen. 29). I will leave this for you to discover. It is a very contemporary, reality story. To say that the sisters were rivals would be an understatement. Each was determined to give Israel an heir and I am sure each did their best to be the first mother. God blessed Leah, it seems, because she was unloved and she had the first four children, all boys (Reuben, Simeon, Levi, and Judah). Both Levi and Judah have prominent parts in this story. Levi's father, from the tribe that produces the priestly line of Israel, and Judah are prophesied to be the line through which the kings will come. Through his line, David and Solomon

26

came. More importantly, Judah's line is Jesus' line through which the King of Kings would be born.

When Rachel's womb is blessed, she births the last two sons to be born to Israel. Her firstborn is Joseph and we know from scripture that God has a purpose and destiny. His name means *"may Jehovah add."* Joseph quickly becomes his father's favorite and, combined with his gift for prophetic dreams, caused his brothers to hate him even more. To add fuel to their hatred, Joseph arrogantly interprets the dreams to his brothers.

So, when his brothers plot to kill the young arrogant dreamer, it is Judah who comes to the rescue and quickly devises a plan that can spare his life and solve the problem. Joseph is sold to a caravan of traders headed for Egypt. God's providence intervenes and Joseph's journey fulfills his destiny, "Yes, you yourselves planned evil against me. God planned it for good in order to bring about what it is this day — to preserve the lives of many people (Gen. 50:20)." Joseph experienced hardship, even prison, but he made it to second in command to Pharaoh because he proved true and faithful to Pharaoh and Yahweh. He saved a nation and his own family from starvation during a great famine. Because of him, his family was readily received and welcomed in Egypt.

The Patriarch is Dying:
CLUE: FOLLOW THE BLESSING

When Israel was near death, he called his sons to his bedside and mostly blessed each son. What is interesting was that he did not go in complete birth order. If you look at the chart, he blessed all of Leah's sons first in birth order, then he blessed all the sons born to handmaidens and lastly, Joseph and Benjamin in birth order. Israel spent the most words on Judah and Joseph, both of whom I spoke about earlier.

Curiously, Israel had a private meeting with Joseph and his sons born in Egypt prior to blessing his sons. Joseph lines the boys up so that all his dad would have to do was put his hands on the boy in front of him. But Israel crosses his hands and blesses the younger Ephraim with his right hand (usually reserved for the older) and the older Manasseh with his left. Joseph frantically strives with his father's hands to no avail. Israel assures him that it is ok and that the younger brother "will become greater" than the older and "his seed will be the fullness of the nations." Then he blessed them that day saying, "In you shall Israel bless, saying: 'May God make you like Ephraim and like Manasseh."

God's ways are mysterious, and the typical rule that the oldest shall receive the birthright is not always the case. Just ask Ishmael and Hagar.

The apportionment of land was done by "allotment" and an actual casting of lots. It was a method by which Joshua and the nation determined God's will. We know not what these "lots" looked like. We know from scripture that the high priests used "Urim & Thummim" to determine God's will (Exodus 28:30). We are told that they were kept within the breastplate of judgment, "on Aaron's heart." What they looked like, we do not know. Lots were cast on the boat that carried Jonah (Jonah 1:7) to determine Judas' replacement, Matthias (Acts 1:26). And they cast lots for Jesus' clothing at His crucifixion (Matthew 27: 35). There are more references to casting lots in scripture; even David appears to prophesy the casting of lots for Jesus' clothes in Psalm 22:19.

Interestingly, the first lot or allotment fell to Judah. Ironic? I think not, as Judah is the Royal Line, through which the Kingly line would be established. Then, both of Joseph's boys come next, Ephraim and then Manasseh just as Israel had prophesied in his blessing.

Did you notice who did not receive land? The tribe of Levi. Why did they not receive land? Joshua 18:7 explains, "But the Levites have no portion among you — for the priesthood of Adonai is their inheritance." How beautiful is that! Yahweh is their portion. May we be able to say the same. They were not earthly bound. They were heavenly bound. Their inheritance was God! They were the early recipients of a Spiritual inheritance. Paul tells the Philippian faith community: *"For our citizenship is in heaven, and from there we eagerly wait for the Savior, the Lord Yeshua the Messiah. He will transform this humble body of ours into the likeness of His glorious body, through the power that enables Him even to put all things in subjection to Himself." Hallelujah!*

I might mention that in the past couple of years in the United States of America, we have heard mention of "sanctuary cities." This is not a new concept and is perhaps copied from scripture. In Joshua 20, six cities were sought out to be "cities of refuge." The belief is that these were Levitical cities to which someone who accidentally and unintentionally killed someone could flee for protection.

Two more observations about the chart. In Ezekiel 48, the prophet tells us that the tribes were apportioned "By Lot" and divinely, Judah is the seventh "Lot" drawn. Seven is, of course, the number of completeness and perfection. There are 7 days in the week, 7 festivals, 7 communities of faith, 7 colors in the rainbow, 7 fruits of the Spirit, and 7 last words of Jesus.

The last column represents the Revelation 7:4-8 passage defining the 144,000 who are marked with a "seal on the forehead of the servants of God." If you take a close look at the passage, some names are missing from the original list and a couple of names have been added as well. The tribes of Dan and Ephraim are missing. Manasseh, the eldest son of Joseph stays, and Joseph replaces Ephraim.

Why are Dan and Ephraim missing? In an article by versebyverseministry.org, dated July 14, 2015, titled, Why is the Tribe of Dan missing in Rev. 7, they state that:

In Judges 17-21, we're given two stories of apostasy in Israel. Both stories center on the tribes of Dan and Ephraim and on the city of Bethlehem, the birthplace of David, God's choice for king over Israel. The writer of Judges emphasizes in these chapters that these were the days before Israel had a king.

In those chapters of Judges, Dan sinned by viewing the land God allotted to them as unacceptable, so they abandoned it. While passing through Ephraim, they stole idols from a home and recruited a Levite to serve in a false temple in the new territory. As a result, Dan became the first tribe in Israel to embrace idol worship in Israel.

Meanwhile, the tribe of Ephraim, the source of the idols, assumed control over the land originally intended for Dan. They aided and abetted the Danites in bringing idolatry into the land of Israel. These sins give just cause for God to exclude them from the privilege of preparing Israel and the world for the Messiah's return.

The Advent of the Judges:
CLUE: DID GOD DO THE APPOINTING?

Before there were kings, God initiated a period in Hebrew history called the Judges. The model that God ordained and gave to the Hebrew nations was prophets, priests (including High Priest), judges, oracles, and seers. The first three were offices that were ordained and anointed as instruments through which He would lead, instruct, guide, and judge His people. God met directly with them.

Early Old Testament examples were Noah, whom God gave instructions to build an ark. He provided him with the scale model of all the dimensions and design and then personally closed the door. To Abraham, He met with him at the burning bush that could not be consumed and the altar on which he was to sacrifice his only begotten son, Isaac. To Moses, He gave the Ten Commandments, the rules governing man's relationship with God and man. To Joshua, He gave the instructions to conquer the land God promised or purposed for them, from assembling the people to cross the Jordan to the instructions for each battle. When Joshua sought and listened to Yahweh, he and the nation were invincible. When they tried to do battle on their own, they lost.

Who were the Judges?

For our purposes and conversation, a judge's primary anointing was as an instrument of deliverance. As a nation, Israel was surrounded by nations who served pagan gods and were hostile to Israel. Israel had a covenant relationship with Yahweh. They were His chosen people; He was their God. Both metaphorically and spiritually, God and Israel were married. Similarly, Jesus is the bridegroom of His New Testament, born-again followers.

Each of the Judges in the book of Judges was tasked with delivering Israel (when they were a united nation) from an oppressor and bringing peace to the land. There was a cycle in every Judge's life, of God raising an oppressor, the oppressor coming across territorial boundaries, oppressing the people, and the people crying out to God (oppression brings us back and closer to God). God would raise a Judge and he or she would militarily defeat the oppressors and restore peace for approximately 40 years. Then, the people would eventually get lazy, compromise their loyalty to God (like us and our marriages or relationship with Him), and fall into sin (embrace idols, idolatry with other non-living, false gods, immorality) and another oppressor arises. The cycle continues.

Do you see any similarities to this dysfunctional cycle of Sin exhibited by the nation of Israel and the sin of our nation and our lives? Therefore, God spoke directly to Solomon in the night with these words: *Thus, Solomon finished the House of Adonai and the king's palace. Indeed, all that Solomon had on his heart to accomplish in the House of Adonai and in his palace, he successfully completed. Then Adonai appeared to Solomon at night and said to him: "I have heard your prayer and have chosen this place for Myself for a House of sacrifice. If I shut up heaven that there is no rain, or if I command the locust to devour the land, or if I send pestilence among My people, when My people, Over whom My Name is called, humble themselves and pray and seek My face and turn from their evil ways, then I will hear from heaven and will forgive their sin and will heal their land. Now My eyes will be open and My ears attentive to*

the prayer offered in this place. For now, I have chosen and consecrated this House so that My Name may be there forever. My eyes and My heart shall be there perpetually. As for you, if you walk before Me as your father David walked, doing all that I have commanded you, keeping My statutes and My ordinances, then I will establish your royal throne as I covenanted with your father, David, saying, 'You shall not lack a man to be ruler in Israel.' But if you turn away and forsake My decrees and My mitzvot that I have set before you, and go and serve other gods and worship them, then I will uproot them from My land which I gave them, and this House which I have consecrated for My Name I will cast out of My sight. I will make it a proverb and a byword among all people. As for this House, which is so exalted, everyone passing by it shall be appalled and say, 'Why has ADONAI done this to this land and to this House?' And they will answer, 'Because they have forsaken ADONAI, the God of their fathers who brought them out of the land of Egypt and clung to other gods, worshipping and serving them. Therefore, He has brought all this misery upon them.'" 2 Chronicles7:11-22

God gave his anointing to the house (temple) that Solomon had built for Yahweh, but he gave Solomon His warning of what would happen if, as a nation, they turned away from Him. We know from the scripture what happened. Just as foreign women turned Solomon's heart away from God, the nation followed suit and God's judgment came. First, the Assyrians in 722 BCE came down from the North and took the northern part of the kingdom into captivity. Then in 598 BCE, the Babylonians destroyed the Temple and plundered the furniture and implements of worship, desecrating the Holy place. What God had prophesied to Solomon took place. The temple was rebuilt in 516/515 BCE.

I want to quote Tamara Cohn Eskenazi, a professor at Hebrew Union College-Jewish Institute of Religion from her article titled: The Destruction and Reconstruction of the Temple:

> *"Whether or not it compared favorably to the first temple, the restored temple marked a new epoch; it signified the renewal of Jewish life after the devastation of exile. Moreover, it signaled a new role for the people themselves. Whereas the first temple was credited to Solomon and was built with forced labor, the second temple was the work of the people themselves. Although it came into being under Persian royal auspices (see Ezra 1:1-4), the actual builders were the Judeans (Ezra 1:5-6:14), who also unilaterally vowed to maintain it (Nehemiah 10:32-39). In the absence of a monarchy, the second temple came to occupy a greater place in Judean life than did Solomon's temple."*

Professor Eskenazi makes two important observations about this period in the history of Israel. The exiles marked the end of the monarchy in Israel and Judah, and the restoration of the Temple marked a new "epoch" of Jewish life and a "new role" for the people.

God pulled down, destroyed the former institution made by a king's hand, and reconstructed another Temple by the hand of the people. God also resorted back to the original model of priest and prophet through Ezra and Jeremiah (see both Biblical books).

Is God possibly doing a similar work today? It is extraordinary that we as people like to build a structure for God, which restricts and puts Him in a box. We build a structure and ask Him to bless and anoint it. We make our own decisions apart from God and we seek His blessing. We construct religion and foist it upon our fellow man that we have the authority and legitimacy to suppress each other.

Why don't we acquiesce to God's model and humble ourselves? We hinder while we are trying to help. As a father, have you ever had your toddler son who wants to get in on the action and help you? He means well, but we all know he gets in the way. We can try to help, and God allows us to 'try,' but we need to learn His ways and model what He models.

Jesus is recorded in John 5:19-21 with these words: "Amen I tell you, the Son cannot do anything by Himself. He can do only what He sees the Father doing. Whatever the Father does, the Son does likewise. For the Father loves the Son and shows Him everything He does. He will show Him even greater works than these so that you will be amazed. For just as the Father raises the dead and gives them life, so also the Son gives life to whomever He wants."

May we come to the place where we only want to do what we see Jesus doing. Just as His Father was His model, Jesus is our model. May we come to do greater things than He. He prophesied it; may it come to pass as we embrace a new identity as His Ekklesia, His new community of faith.

The Advent of a king
CLUE: Man thinks he has a better plan

If the Hebrew nation operated under a Theocracy, then how did they transition to living under a king? We find the answer in 1 Samuel 8. The Hebrew nation had looked around at all the surrounding nations and noticed that they had a king. Isn't it human nature to desire what our neighbors have? Since national identity is fueled by individual identity, they opted for the same style of government.

Imagine turning your back on God after all he has done for you. Most of us have. They were no different. If we only go back in history to their enslavement in Egypt, the miracles that God performed right in their midst, we see that they quickly forgot. Fickle-minded like us, they quickly got selective amnesia.

They remembered fondly the "the fish, which they used to eat for free, the cucumbers, the melons, the leeks, the onions, and the garlic! But now we have no appetite. We never see anything but this manna (Num. 11:5)."

One by one, God had eliminated the gods of Egypt. Which one would you have preferred if you were them? Would you prefer blood-filled rivers (so nasty that all the fish die and begin rotting; frogs on everything and they begin rotting; gnats everywhere; flies in swarms; livestock die; boils all over your body and on animals; hail so violent that it would kill whatever was not indoors and decimate crops; locusts eating all your crops; darkness "that may be felt (Ex. 10:21b) or a death angel? In one night, Yahweh demonstrates Himself in a death blow upon the firstborn of the Egyptians and their animals.

I have heard scientists try to explain away how this could happen via natural phenomena. What they conveniently miss is that none of these plagues touched the Hebrew children, or their children, or their crops, or their animals. How do you explain that other than that God has pinpoint accuracy? He had laser-guided accuracy before man even dreamt of it.

Generations come and generations go.

The Hebrews as a nation had an extensive oral tradition and the worship of Yahweh was their entire lifestyle and yet they forgot. They had a feast to commemorate these acts of God so they would not forget. They were given the Torah in the wilderness to help them remember and still they forgot. God had to allow a whole generation to die off so He could raise a new generation who would have the confidence in God to fulfill His covenant and take them into the Promised Land.

Joshua, which means "Yahweh delivered", and who was the servant of Moses, became the new leader. And so, He did through Joshua and Caleb, the only two spies to believe they could take the land.

It is difficult for me to imagine why they would choose a king over God's man, God's way, a Theocracy. What is it within man that we look upon others and want what they have, and we want to blend in? It shows such a blatant disregard for who God is. God tells Samuel they are rejecting Me, not you.

I told you that there was a period of Judges. That period, that season was coming to an end. Why? Well, we are told that Samuel had two sons, Joel and Abijah. On their fathers' coattails, they both became judges and they forsook their father's ways and compromised and became corrupt. They went after "dishonest gain," meaning that they received money under the table for a favorable ruling. "They took bribes and perverted justice (1 Sam. 8:1-3)."

Parents, including Samuel, were not able to keep their sons in line. If you have adult children who are not living for the Lord, First Place Ministries has an International Prayer call via Zoom, directed at families and children, especially adult children. We desire to come alongside you while we battle in the Spirit together for their reconciliation with God and then you.

Take heart—there are plenty of dysfunctional families in the Bible. There are plenty of examples of children who were defiant, angry, scheming, and left home to tour the world. We want to walk with you and contend for their return.

So, the Hebrew nation had had enough torment, abuse, and war with neighboring nations. They wanted a king like all the other nations. So, God gave them what they wanted.

There were good kings and bad kings.

Refer to this chart of the Kings of Israel, Good Kings, Evil Kings –https://www.providenceacademy.org/wp-content/uploads/2020/01/Chart-of-the-Kings-of-Israel-and-Judah.pdf

CHAPTER 4

YOU DON'T REFUSE THE KING!
OR THE QUEEN!

Daniel 3:18b: "We will not serve your gods nor worship the golden image that you set up."

1 Samuel 20:32: But Jonathan answered his father Saul, "Why should he be put to death? What has he (David) done?"

1 Kings 18:10b: "I alone am left, and they are seeking my life to take it!"

Esther 4: 16b: "So if I perish, I perish."

Matthew 14:4: Because John had been telling him (Herod), "It is not permitted for you to have her."

> CLUE: There were godly kings and ungodly kings:
> How did godly people respond to each?

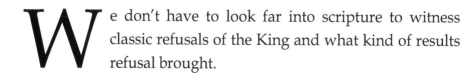

We don't have to look far into scripture to witness classic refusals of the King and what kind of results refusal brought.

Daniel was among the choicest of the exiled youth who were taken to Babylon. But he and his friends stayed true to the God of Israel and said no to the king. *David* wanted to know if Saul could be trusted. Were it not for Jonathan, David might not have survived. He said yes to Adonai at a vital time in Hebrew history. *Elijah* had the courage to pose a question, issue a challenge, backed by a contest between Yahweh and the false gods of Baal and the Asherim. He said "yes," and Elohim responded with a supernatural fire that "consumed the burnt offering –and the wood, the stones, and the dust—and licked up the water in the trench." *Esther* listened to her uncle, Mordecai, and won the king's heart. The former queen refused to dance for the king and she lost her crown. Providentially, Esther was positioned for such a time to save her people. She said "yes" when it counted. *John the Immerser* chose to speak out about Herod having his brother's wife, Herodias. She had a grudge against John and that grudge cost John his life. He said "no" to the king and "yes" to the King of Kings.

> *CLUE: It may cost you (your life) to say "no"*
> *to the king and say "yes" to the King of Kings.*
> *Will you bow down to other gods?*

Daniel and his Jewish friends (Hananiah, Mishael, and Azariah) stood up to the King's servant regarding their diet, which was imposed on them, and survived with raving revues (Daniel 1:5-16). This event alone probably built their faith, so they raised the bar. Later in their exile, the King had a golden image erected, which was "sixty cubits high and six cubits wide." The people of "nations and languages" were to bow down to this image every time they heard music played. Noncompliance would be met with the penalty of death by being "thrown into a fiery furnace." It was observed by those appointed over Daniels' friends that they "pay no heed to you, O king. They do not serve your gods nor will they worship the golden image that you have set up."

You see, the real issue was not disobedience for the sake of being a rebel or non-compliant. The issue was that Daniel and his friends would not bow down to pagan gods. They served only one God, Jehovah. We have lost sight of this central issue in our compliance or noncompliance with today's government orders. If only you knew the gods that our elites and people in government on both sides of the aisles, heads of states, and nations serve. It is very blatant and obvious.

If you are not aware of the whole story, they did get thrown into the fiery furnace and emerged unscathed. In fact, the king was so angry that just for these boys, they stoked the fire to a 7x greater temperature. It was so hot it killed the men who escorted the boys to throw them into the fire.

The king enjoyed watching his evil work from a viewing stand, which gave him a viewing into the fire. The king is characterized as "astonished and leaping to his feet." He couldn't believe his eyes. "Four men (were) walking about unbound and unharmed in the middle of the fire, and the fourth has the appearance like a son of the gods (Daniel 3:19-25)."

Do we have men and women with the faith of Daniel and his friends? People who say, "Our God whom we serve is able to

43

save us from the furnace of blazing fire and He will deliver us out of your hand, O king. Yet even if He does not, let it be known to you, O king, that we will not serve your gods nor worship the golden image that you set up."

I propose that the fourth person was either God or an angel of God. He was with them in the fire and saw them through the fire. Not only were they unscathed and unharmed, but there was also no hint of smell of smoke on their clothes! "The fire had no effect on the bodies of these men. Not a hair of their head was singed, nor were their robes scorched, nor was there a smell of fire on them (Daniel 3: 27b)." I have been around plenty of campfires and never have I been able to avoid smelling like smoke. This was a divine intervention by the Almighty God!

Where is our Daniel's, Shadrach's, Meshach's, and Abed-Nego's? Will God not do the same today! I have heard our preachers teach on John 14:12-14 with great conviction. Where are you today, brothers? From our collective inaction, I sense that you are saying, "I am willing to stand up; just do not ask me to stand against the narrative of the government, the popular narrative of the world, or institutional powers. I encourage you with these words: *"Amen, amen I tell you. He who puts his trust in Me, the works that I do he will do; and greater than these he will do, because I am going to the Father. And whatever you ask in My name, that I will do, so that the Father may be glorified in the Son. If you ask Me anything in My name, I will do it." John 14:12-14*

Will you dare to contest against evil?
Even if you garner the wrath of the queen?
CLUE: WHAT FORCES DID ELIJAH STAND AGAINST?

There is a prophet we used to boast about in sermons and teach children in Sunday School because he had the hutzpah to challenge the false prophets of Baal (1 Kings 18:20-40).

The issue Elijah announced seems very contemporary in nature. "How long will you waver between two opinions? If Adonai is God, follow Him, but if Baal is, follow him." The problem we face is that the enemy is not that clear-cut. Many Christians and Pastors do not see our current situation as being a demonic battle. We are too busy being distracted and seeing two parties. We do not see the big picture and we have embraced the narrative of the world rather than declaring the narrative of God's word. We have taken the narrative of social issues and Christianized them. I have not heard one pastor resolve the social justice issue with one verse. Matthew 7: 12: "So in all things, do to others what you would want them to do to you—for this is the Torah and the Prophets." There is no color represented in this passage. There is no favoritism represented. There is no discrimination. Simply good old-fashioned Godly wisdom and common sense.

I want to introduce you to a man who I heard speak recently. His name is Shahram Hadian. He is an Iranian-born Muslim. He is a born-again Christian. His father was in the military and by his testimony, his father was an advancement away from becoming a General. It was at that time that his father knew the signs of

Shah's fall from power and he quickly escaped with his father and family.

I recently met another man who was raised in El Salvador and escaped the communist takeover. I met a Romanian woman a couple of years ago whose father was also in the military. They had wealth in Romania and left it all to escape a dictator.

Each of them understands the signs and wonders; how come Americans cannot see it? I tell them that we do not think it could happen to America.

In the late seventies, I traveled to Southern California to attend Biola University. We lived near Disney Land, so naturally when grandparents came to visit, they would take their grandchildren to Disney Land. I will never forget one exhibit that had a robotic Abraham Lincoln. He stood up and addressed the audience. During that speech, he made a statement that I will never forget. To paraphrase, he said, "America will never be overtaken from forces outside the nation. If America falls, it will be from within." How prophetic those words are today.

Do we care enough to stand up and turn it around?

I know this is not going to be popular and I am not proposing this action or response. If one reads the rest of the account of this supernatural contest on Mount Carmel, there was revival! Everyone "fell on their faces and they said, "Adonai, He is God! Adonai, He is God!"

And then, Elijah eradicated the land of false prophets. He took every one of them hostage. The passage doesn't give us a lot of detail other than that he asked for help to "seize the prophets of Baal! Let not a single one of them escape." It seems that he alone slew every one of them. Do you remember how many prophets of Baal Elijah squared off with? 450 to 1, or 850 to 1. (If we read the full text, there were also 400 prophets of Asherah vs. 19). What kind of odds do you think Las Vegas would have given to Elijah? He felt that he was the lone "prophet of Adonai left."

I assume that our pastors listened to the news of our pastors to the north in Canada who were arrested during the lockdowns. The sad report I read from an interview with Pastor Artur Pawlowski of the Fortress (Cave) of Adullam Church in Alberta, Canada was that "not a single pastor came to visit him in the jail". He felt like he was on his own. No pastoral support of any kind. I told a pastor friend recently that I feel that our pastors in America have been defanged, declawed, and wearing pink.

Like my friends I mentioned before, he also escaped from the communist takeover. So, he gets it and is willing to take a stand. We must take a stand. Sitting pat and doing nothing or being silent is no longer an option.

> *I am coming to you in the name of Adonai-Tzva'ot,*
> *God of the armies of Israel, whom you have defied."*
> **CLUE: Did David stand against a human enemy only?**
> **Or were spiritual forces present?**

David knew the identity of the enemy of God and Israel. He not only had supreme confidence from killing both a lion and a bear (1 Samuel 17: 36), he also had supreme faith in the God of Israel.

47

Imagine a young boy, an older adolescent or younger teenager, bringing his older brother's food at the battle line and observing cowardice. Imagine his offense at the giant's taunts and complete disregard and disrespect of the God of Israel. For forty days, both armies had been posturing against each other and each day, the giant came out to the front of the line and "defied" that army of Israel to select one soldier to fight mano-a-mano. The victor would win for his nation and the loser would serve the other. The loser's nation would become the victor's slave. The text tells us, "They (the soldiers of Israel) were dismayed and terrified (vs.11)." They were totally intimidated. This giant was reputed to be over 9" tall and wielding a spear over 15 lbs. in weight. He also sported a shield-bearer who marched ahead of him.

It was the physical mixed with the psychological warfare that decimated the army of Israel. It was the audacity and attitude that galled David. How arrogant of this uncircumcised Philistine to taunt and "defy the ranks of the living God (vs.26)?" David was so confident, so assured that God would deliver him from the hand of the Philistine. He told Saul of his conquests in protecting his father's flocks. "Your servant has killed both the lion and the bear, so this uncircumcised Philistine will become like one of them — since he has defied the ranks of the living God (vs. 36)."

Saul was convinced and said, "Go, and may Adonai be with you (vs. 37b)." But just to be sure, Saul tried dressing David in all the implements of war. He tried on a "bronze helmet," and he tried on the full-body "armor". He tried walking in the armor. Can you imagine? It was awkward and mechanical. David was used to being nimble and fluid — unencumbered and mobile. This gear made him neither.

David chose the weapons he had used to protect the flock: "With his staff and five smooth stones, he put them in the pocket of his shepherd's bag that he had, and with his sling in his hand, he approached the Philistine (vs. 40)."

The smirk on the face of the overconfident Philistine could not be hidden. This was too good to be true. This is game over. I have won! He was so confident; he continued his tirade of trash talking! "Am I a dog that you come to me with sticks? Then the Philistine cursed David by his gods. He said to David, "Come to me so I may give your flesh to the birds of the sky and the beasts of the field."

He sounds demonic, doesn't he? He was. He had cursed David with his false gods. David came to him in the name of Jehovah God and prevailed. He said Yes to Adonai and no to the devil.

Then David said to the Philistine, "You are coming to me with a sword, a spear, and a javelin, but I am coming to you in the Name of ADONAI-Tzva'ot, God of the armies of Israel, whom you have defied. This very day, ADONAI will deliver you into my hand and I will strike you down and take your head off you, and I will give the carcasses of the Philistines' camp today to the birds of the sky and the wild beasts of the earth. Then all the earth will know that there is a God in Israel, and so all this assembly will know that ADONAI delivers not with sword and spear—for the battle belongs to ADONAI—and He will give you into our hands." 1 Samuel 17: 45-47

We know the rest of the story from our years of Sunday school. David ran toward the giant, bold and unafraid. He reached into his bag and pulled out a stone. He placed it in the pocket of his sling and wound up, took aim and, with the strength of the Lord, released a volley that struck the giant between the eyes and sunk into his forehead. He may have staggered for a moment but then he fell "on his face to the ground." In that moment, fear drained from the army of Israel and they faced the army of the Philistines. In that instant, everything changed. Both armies ran! David ran and took Goliath's sword and cut off his head, raising it in victory. He not only killed the enemy of the living God, but he also silenced the defiant Philistine and demoralized an entire nation. With that act, he empowered an entire army and emboldened a nation. He elevated the faith of Israel in Adonai-Tzva'ot, God of the armies of Israel.

One man's faith in Adonai-Tzva'ot has been spoken about for centuries. See what God can do through just one who would believe that He can deliver us from the loud, boisterous, cursing, defiant, lying, overconfident, intimidating, arrogant, fearmongering mouth of our enemy.

The army of Israel ran for the enemy soldiers and slew the Philistine soldiers all the way back home to the gates of Ekron. Then the Bnei-Yisrael returned from chasing the Philistines to plunder their camp.

David victoriously carries the head of Goliath all the way to Jerusalem. The text tells us that he was escorted by Abner, the commander of the army, and "brought before Saul the head of the Philistine in his hand." Saul was curious about whose son this was. Somehow in the heat of battle, whose son this was had escaped him. David answers, "I am the son of your servant, Jesse the Beth-lehemite (vs. 58)."

David solved the immediate problem by silencing and taking the voice of the enemy away from the Philistines. But they were not eradicated. They would be back and be a thorn in Saul and David's lives.

KNOW YOUR ENEMY!
CLUE: DID GOD IDENTIFY THE ENEMY?

We must understand and know our enemy. The Scripture gives us a lot of information about our accuser and enemy of our soul, Satan. We are told he is a:

A murderer & liar and the father of all lies	John 8:44
Accuser of brothers and sisters	Rev. 12:10
A thief (who) comes to steal, slaughter, and destroy	John 10:10
A schemer, wicked, power of darkness, flaming arrows	Eph. 6:10-20
A roaring lion, seeking someone to devour	1 Pet. 5:8

The devil, Satan is not tame, is not gentle; he seeks your demise. If there is ever a time to understand and identify your enemy, it is today. The agenda of the powers of this world is to reduce our numbers, Christian or non-Christian, Muslim, or Jew, black or white, gay, or straight. He does not care what the method is, whether it is self-induced or mandated.

I want to share an observation I made a couple of years ago about the "temptation of Jesus." Most of us can recite that Jesus faced three recorded temptations and He answered Satan with three different scriptures, quoting the word of God in rebuking and rebuffing him. And we walk away from the passage satisfied that we have received all we need to know about Jesus' temptation experience. But read vs. 13: "And when the devil had completed every test, he departed from Him until another occasion." Some translations say "an opportune time". What this tells me is that even though he called it a day, he was not through with Jesus or us. He has been awaiting opportune times or other occasions throughout history. And I want to elaborate on some other opportune times throughout history and I believe today, right now, is one of those occasions. Never has mankind been under assault in so many varied ways as we are right now.

CLUE: Did our enemy leave the universe after tempting Jesus?

If I can encourage you in any way today, it is to know who your enemy is. Get acquainted with Ephesians 6:10-20 and then suit up every day! Even during peacetime, our military puts on their uniform, their battle gear, every day. David tried it on, but never having worn it before, now, at the moment of battle was not the time to familiarize himself with the armor. I encourage you to not only dress for battle every day but to give heed to vs. 18:

"Pray in the Ruach on every occasion, with all kinds of prayers and requests." Regardless of your persuasion about the Spirit, now is the time to engage in the Spirit. Doing the command of this verse will take your prayer life to another dimension. Know that the two verses before Romans 8:28, which you all know, say this: *In the same way, the Ruach helps in our weakness. For we do not know how to pray as we should, but the Ruach Himself intercedes for us with groans too deep for words. And He who searches the hearts knows the mind of the Ruach because He intercedes for the kedoshim according to the will of God. Now we know that all things work together for good for those who love God, who are called according to His purpose.*

What an empowerment to know that the Holy Spirit is praying for us according to the will of God! Many times we do not know how to pray and what to say. When these times come, there is no better option than to pray in the Spirit! Your pastor can preach against this all he wants, but he is remiss, is preaching error, and needs to repent! Pray for him or her to receive the Holy Spirit and watch the newfound "power" they will receive according to Acts 1:8!

> *"But you will receive power when the Ruach ha-Kodesh has come upon you; and you will be My witnesses in Jerusalem, and through all Judah, and Samaria, and to the end of the earth."*

I hope that by now you are beginning to say, yes, I would say "no" to the king and "Yes to the King of Kings!"

CHAPTER 5

WHAT WERE THE KING'S (JAMES') INFLUENCES ON THE KING JAMES BIBLE? AGAIN, WHO WOULD SAY NO TO THE KING?

"Most Germans had no idea that Hitler, in fact, despised Christianity. He thought it a weak religion, and he desperately wished that Germany could be rid of it as soon as possible. Of course, he could never say this publicly since most Germans thought of themselves as good Lutheran Christians. So Hitler pretended to be a Christian because he knew that saying what he really believed would erode his political power. Hitler's goal was to slowly infiltrate the church with Nazi ideology and take over it from the inside. He wanted to unify all the German churches and create a single state church that submitted to him alone. But he would do it a step at a time to avoid drawing attention to his efforts. And like the proverbial frog in the pot of boiling water, the German people would not realize what was happening until it was too late." Eric Metaxas, 7 Men and the secret of their greatness pg. 101 Chapter 4, Dietrich Bonhoeffer.

"I testify to everyone who hears the words of the prophecy of this book. If anyone adds to them, God shall add to him the plagues that are written in this book; and if anyone takes away from the words of the book of this prophecy, God shall take away his share in the Tree of Life and the Holy City, which are written in this book." Revelation 22:18-19

Throughout history, we see examples of kings who wanted to establish a name—a legacy—for themselves. The first that comes to mind is King David. He wanted to build a house for God. He had a nice house; Yahweh was certainly worthy of His own house. It was a noble idea, but it was another example of man trying to accommodate and contain God. Yahweh's instructions were for the Tent of Meeting. Great definitions and instructions were given to the Hebrew nation. When Yahweh moved, the tent was moved. God was mobile! Not static.

While David was not allowed to build the temple because he was a man of bloodshed, he was allowed to design, draw up the plans, and acquire the materials used to build the Temple. Certainly, the accomplishments of King David cemented his place as the preeminent earthly king of Israel.

It is not uncommon for kings to want to leave a legacy.

From John Rampton, who is the co-founder and CEO of Calendar, here is an example from information on the Julian Calendar: *"The new calendar spread across the empire and also into neighboring states and client kingdoms, where calendars became 365 days with one leap day, initially every three years but eventually every four years.*

"The names of the previous months remained mostly unchanged. January honored the god, Janus who symbolizes "new beginnings". These gods are interesting to study for many reasons, but the god Janus had one head, but two faces. In honor of this god, one face could look forward to the future, and one face looked back to the previous year. Every month had deep reflections, thoughts, concerns, and deliberations to come to a consensus of opinions. The calendar was vastly serious to these people.

February is likely to derive from the Februa festival. March was for the god, Mars. The origins of April, May, and June are unclear, but they may have been derived from the Etruscan god Apru and the gods, Maia and Juno, respectively. An alternative theory is that April comes from the Latin word "aperire," which means to open, while May and June are old terms for "senior" and "junior."

The remaining months were named after their order in the calendar. Quintilis was the fifth month; Sextilis, the sixth; September, the seventh; October, the eighth; November, the ninth; and December, the tenth. The Julian reform pushed the months down the calendar so that December became the twelfth month without changing its name. Quintilis, however, the birth month of Julius Caesar became Iulius ("July" in English) and Sextilis became Augustus or August.

Other emperors tried to rename months too. Caligula tried to call September "Germanicus" to honor his father. Nero wanted April to be called "Neroneus". Domitian wanted October to become "Domitianus". These names didn't stick.

Note the information of various kings who wanted to rename months for either themselves or a family member. Consider Julius Caesar and Caesar Augustus.

Days of the weeks have been named after various false gods like the sun-god (Sunday) and moon-god (Monday). Has it dawned on you how conditioned we are to use a calendar that honors false deity? We drive cars named after false deities, planets, and celestial bodies. Names like Equinox, Geo, Saturn, Mercury, Subaru, Solstice, Celica, Eclipse, Taurus, and Galaxy.

So why would it seem to be beyond suspicion that a king in England, who commissioned an English translation to be made, would not influence a few key changes to the Bible? What kind of influences would a king exert?

Setting the Stage: Who is King James?
CLUE: Could King James have been influenced by Satan?

King James was born in Edinburgh, Scotland.

The Puritans were eager to continue the work of the Reformation, and the death of Elizabeth seemed their opportune moment. Scotland's James VI succeeded her, thus becoming James I of England. Because James had been raised under Presbyterian influences, the Puritans had reason to expect that James would champion their cause. They were gravely mistaken.

James was acquainted with many of their kind in Scotland, and he did not like them. However, they were a sizeable minority, serious, well educated, highly motivated, and convinced of the righteousness of their convictions. Regardless of personal antipathy, James did not consider it politically wise to ignore them.

The Presbyterians wanted to do away with the hierarchical structure of powerful bishops. They advanced what they believed was the New Testament model of church administration under elders or presbyters. The Nonconformists and Separatists, some of whom would later become America's Pilgrims, wanted the state out of church affairs altogether.

Then there was Parliament—eager to expand its power beyond the role it had at the time. There was a significant Puritan influence and representation in the Parliament.

To keep our alliteration, let's refer to the next group as the "Prayer Book" establishment or the Bishops and the hierarchy of the English church. They were a genuine elite, holding exceptional power, privilege, and wealth. To them, Puritan agitation was far more than an intellectual abstraction to be debated at Oxford and Cambridge. If the Puritans were to prevail, this hierarchy had much to lose.

You can see the battle lines being drawn. The king must seize control of the situation. Not long after, the Puritans submitted a document to the king, which became known as the Millenary Petition. It had 4 areas of concern ranging from "Church services, Church ministry, Church livings and maintenance, and Church discipline". So, the king's response was to prepare a conference led by him and attended by his "Privy Council of Advisors, nine bishops and deans, and four moderate representatives of the Puritan cause". Professor Curtis notes that "the deck was stacked against the Puritans. The Puritan delegation was not allowed to attend the first day of conference, which presented the opening remarks in a speech given by the king."

At the conference, Dr. John Reynolds, head of Corpus Christi College, gave the Puritan response and mentioned "broadening the decision-making base by including the presbytery." He had crossed the line. The last thing the king wanted to do was to share the decision-making process with anyone else.

At this point, he warned Reynolds: "If this be all your party hath to say, I will make them conform themselves, or else I will harrie them out of the land, or else do worse!"

While Reynolds' unfortunate use of the term presbytery damaged the Puritan case, he does get credit for proposing the most significant achievement of the conference. Reynolds "informed his majesty that there might be a new translation of the Bible because those that were allowed in the reign of King Henry VIII and King Edward VI were corrupt and not answerable to the truth of the original." James accepted the idea of a new translation because he despised the then-popular Geneva Bible.

King James liked the idea of a new English Translation for several reasons, but most of all, it established his control and authority. He strengthened his relationship with the finest seminaries England boasted in Oxford, Cambridge, and Westminster. He also tightened his grip as the head of the Church of England.

(Excerpts taken from an article on Christianity.com, titled Story Behind King James Bible by Dr. Ken Curtis, PH. D, April 28, 2010.)

CHAPTER 6

IT WAS A SOFT COUP. WHAT A KING ESTABLISHED WITH THE STROKE OF A PEN AND THE ASSISTANCE OF ENGLAND'S FINEST THEOLOGIANS.

"Implicit in Christ's words, 'My Ekklesia,' is a threat to every corrupt human government and demonic principality." Dean Briggs (pg. 120, Ekklesia Rising)

"Cross-bearing is the original version of civil disobedience. It is a Christian's submission to the higher law of God, a deliberate rejection of the immoral laws of the state, and a joyful acceptance of the consequences of the stand." Vishal Mangalwadi, Truth and Transformation pg. 185

"I testify to everyone who hears the words of the prophecy of this book. If anyone adds to them, God shall add to him the plagues that are written in this book; and if anyone takes away from the words of the book of this prophecy, God shall take away his share in the Tree of Life and the Holy City, which are written in this book." Revelation 22:18-19

Without a shot, without violence, the Puritans, Anglicans, Bishops, and deans got what they wished for—an English Translation they believed to be authorized on the authority of the king, but not The King. I don't think they realized what they had done. It is much like the scriptural history of the Hebrew nation asking Samuel for a King. They didn't fully understand that what they had wished for was not in their best interest or generations to follow.

I made a comment earlier in this book about the Testing of Jesus by Satan in the wilderness. At the conclusion of the passage (Luke 4:13), the good doctor and writer Luke, uses the phrase "another occasion," which also translates to 'an opportune time.' This moment in history was "another occasion". Many times, our enemy works through someone, using someone to do his bidding and scheming. We are naïve to think he has done everything possible to undermine and sabotage the community of faith.

> **CLUE: Could seminary theologians be influenced by a king or Satan to compromise the scriptures?**

If the seminary-trained theologians who did the king's bidding didn't know, they should have. Changing the wording of Matthew 16:18 from "Ekklesia" to "church" was intentional for the purpose of controlling the faith community, and it has for centuries.

Even though the Puritans eventually left and came to America, they unknowingly brought with them a compromised translation of the Bible. The illusion was freedom. They were still slaves of the king.

It is fascinating to see the ways that England has continued to keep its grip on America though thousands of miles separate us.

If you stand back and observe, it is like a dysfunctional family whose children left home, struggled for independence, yet the parents still extended and exerted power and control in all facets of their lives.

When we have been bankrupt, who did we run back to? The bankers in London, England. They have kept us enslaved for decades if not centuries. Most Americans don't know that we are slaves of a few royal families. How have they enslaved us? Here is an assignment. On your computer, on any browser, type in: "What does it mean when my name on my birth certificate (driver's license, passport) is in ALL CAPITAL LETTERS? There are many sites, so that is why I did not give you a link.

We have been lied to and deceived for centuries. It is timely how all the deception and lies are being exposed and it is interesting how they all, in every category, lead back to England and Rome. Happy hunting!

The New Translation Launched

King James contracted with nearly fifty of the seminary professors. He drafted a document that established the guidelines and requirements of the new translation. It contained 15 Rules of

Translation for The King James Version (KJV). **For our purposes, we will focus on #3** (which I will emphasize with a **bold font** below). "The Old Ecclesiastical Words to be kept, viz. the Word "Church" not to be translated to Congregation.

For your reference, the following segment regarding the "15 Rules of Translation for the King James (KJV)" is entirely taken from this webpage:

https://www.petergoeman.com/15-rules-of-translation-for-the-king-james-version-kjv/

15 Rules of Translation for the King James Version (KJV)

When King James commissioned the King James Version, he approved 15 principles of translation that were instituted by Richard Bancroft, the bishop of London in 1604. These translation principles are as follows:

1. *The ordinary Bible read in the Church, commonly called the Bishop's Bible, is to be followed, and as little altered as the Truth of the original will permit.*
2. *The names of the Prophets and the Holy Writers, with the other Names of the Text, to be retained, as nigh as may be, accordingly as they were vulgarly used.*
3. **The Old Ecclesiastical Words to be kept, viz. the Word Church not to be translated to Congregation.**
4. *When a Word hath diverse Significations, that to be kept which hath been most commonly used by the most of the Ancient Fathers, being agreeable to the Propriety of the Place, and the Analogy of the Faith.*

64

5. *The Division of the Chapters to be altered, either not at all, or as little as may be, if Necessity so require.*

6. *No Marginal Notes at all to be affixed, but only for the explanation of the Hebrew or Greek Words, which cannot without some circumlocution, so briefly and fitly be expressed in the Text.*

7. *Such Quotations of Places to be marginally set down as shall serve for the fit Reference of one Scripture to another.*

8. *Every particular Man of each Company, to take the same Chapter or Chapters, and having translated or amended them severally by himself, where he thinketh good, all to meet together, confer what they have done, and agree for their Parts what shall stand.*

9. *As any one Company hath dispatched any one Book in this Manner, they shall send it to the rest, to be considered of seriously and judiciously, for His Majesty is very careful in this Point.*

10. *If any Company, upon the Review of the Book so sent, doubt or differ upon any Place, to send them Word thereof; note the Place, and withal send the Reasons, to which if they consent not, the Difference to be compounded at the general Meeting, which is to be of the chief Persons of each Company, at the end of the Work.*

11. *When any Place of special Obscurity is doubted of Letters to be directed by Authority, to send to any Learned Man in the Land, for his Judgment of such a Place.*

12. *Letters to be sent from every Bishop to the rest of his Clergy, admonishing them of this Translation in hand; and to move and charge as many skillful in the Tongues; and having taken pains*

in that kind, to send his particular Observations to the Company, either at Westminster, Cambridge, or Oxford.

13. *The Directors in each Company, to be the Deans of Westminster, and Chester for that Place; and the King's Professors in the Hebrew or Greek in either University.*

14. *These translations to be used when they agree better with the Text than the Bishop's Bible: Tyndale's, Matthew's, Coverdale's, Whitchurch's, Geneva.*

15. *Besides the said Directors before mentioned, three or four of the most Ancient and Grave Divines, in either of the Universities, not employed in Translating, to be assigned by the vice-Chancellor, upon Conference with the rest of the Heads, to be Overseers of the Translations as well Hebrew as Greek, for the better observation of the 4th Rule above specified.*

Translation rules 1, 6, and 14 are interesting. Rule #1 mandated that their translation uses the Bishop's Bible as a base text whenever possible. This was likely because the Bishop's translation was the official Bible of the Church. However, Tyndale's translation ended up being far more influential, accounting for 4/5 (80%) of the KJV New Testament.

Rule #6 mandated no study notes in the margins of the new translation. The Geneva Bible (which was the most popular English translation of the time) had many marginal notations, some of which King James read as challenges to his royal authority. This was the main motivation for a new translation. Thus, the KJV translation was limited from study notes.

Translation rule #14 gives further evidence for the fact that the intention was for the KJV translation to be more of a revision of existing English translations than a new translation. The translators utilized the existing English texts where possible.

Against those who claim the KJV translation is inspired, I have written about how the KJV is not without error. Here, we also note that the KJV itself was not a revolutionary translation. Rather, it was largely a compilation of already existing translations.

"Ekklesia" is the declaration of Jesus
CLUE: WHAT DID JESUS DECLARE?

Let's begin with Matthew 16:18. This passage is my key battleground because, my assertion is, the king had an agenda and he exerted his influence upon the translators to use his word for Ekklesia, namely "church." Why would he do this? He wanted unfettered control and the term "church" accomplished this purpose.

How so? Let's begin with his relationship with the church. King James was the head of the Church of England. *Ekklesia is defined as the called-out Saints and those who are to be a ruling body, a ruling government.* The king didn't want opposition to his rule. He wanted compliance and control. I don't fault the king for wanting control. I fault the theologians who complied with the king and made this little, meaningful change. Understandably, while the theologians were from the best Seminaries England had to offer—Cambridge, Oxford, and Westminster—they were also members of the king's church.

Named for himself

Secondly, he had the Bible named after him. Four hundred years later, we don't even blink an eye. It is just a name we have become used to. We have been told so many times over our lifetime that this translation is the most authoritarian translation available. Sadly, most other translations are based on King James Version. Another sleight of hand move was the translation change from the Hebrew Jacob to the accepted English name, James. While it was accepted before this change and used for his translation, the English equivalent of Jacob is "James." How conveniently deceptive to install your name as one of the book's authors and the title of the Bible.

The king was also an educated man. Here is an overview of his life in an article titled, "James 1" by David Mathew, July 20, 1998 (multiple revisions), "James I, (born June 19, 1566, Edinburgh, Scotland—died March 27, 1625, Theobalds, Hertfordshire, England), king of Scotland (as James VI) from 1567 to 1625 and first Stuart king of England from 1603 to 1625, who styled himself as "King of Great Britain." James was a strong advocate of royal absolutism and his conflicts with an increasingly self-assertive Parliament set the stage for the rebellion against his successor, Charles I.

From this same article, David Mathews concludes: "Besides the political problems that he bequeathed to his son Charles, James left a body of writings, which, though of mediocre quality as literature, entitle him to a unique place among English kings since the time of Alfred. Chief among these writings are two political treatises, The True Law of Free Monarchies (1598) and Basilikon Doron (1599), in which he expounded his own views on the divine right of kings. The 1616 edition of the political works of James I was edited by Charles Howard McIlwain (1918). The Poems of James VI of Scotland (2 vol.) was edited by James Craigie (1955–58). In addition, James famously oversaw a new authorized English translation of the Bible, published in 1611, which became known as the King James Version.

The Divine Right of Kings

Notice that King James wrote a couple of books during the time of the newly translated Bible. The titles alone should cause the most educated of our theological trained seminarians and pastors to raise an eyebrow. They were written to establish the sovereignty of the crown. Really? It seems apparent to me that the king's end game was to establish control of the Church of England as he already had the Church of Scotland.

The battle between the Catholic Church, the Vatican, and the new Church of England appears to me to be one of a transition of power. What is the difference if we have a Pope declaring sovereignty or a King doing the same? While we have not had an official king of the Church installed over the years, King James' reach has been extended from the grave for over 400 years. We have continued over that period to propagate the use of the term "church" because their top theologians complied with the wishes of a king rather than follow the dictate of Jesus, declared in Matthew 16:18.

When Jesus said "Ekklesia," He was uttering a common term that everyone within hearing distance, and in that time period, would understand the meaning: "A governing, ruling body." The best theologians are complicit in compromising the word of God. I fear for their souls based on Revelation 22:18-19: *"I testify to everyone who hears the words of the prophecy of this book. If anyone adds to them, God shall add to him the plagues that are written in this book; and if anyone takes away from the words of the book of this prophecy, God shall take away his share in the Tree of Life and the Holy City, which are written in this book."*

There may be those saying that I am overstating the case. My response to you is the same words Jesus gave Peter, *"Flesh and blood have not revealed this to you, but My Father who is in heaven"* (Matt. 16:17).

This is not my own creation. This process has been percolating for over 15 years. Seven years ago, the dissatisfaction with the institutional church was beginning to churn in my heart. I didn't understand it then, but it is extremely clear to me now.

We have continued to propagate what we were told 400 years ago. We have followed and defended what our fathers told us, and what their fathers were told by their fathers. We didn't challenge it because our fathers and pastors would not lie to us, and I am not charging them with lying to us. I am perplexed though. How come for centuries now, seemingly, no one has challenged what the king accomplished back in the early 1600s? Why didn't (at least we do not know of any dissension) any of the New Testament Translators speak up about the changes made throughout the Bible, especially Matthew 16:18?

However, all it takes is a lie, a half-truth, a calculated change of one word and we are on a course that was and will never be blessed by Jehovah God. It is not and was not His design and never will be. I allege that the simple change of Ekklesia to church set us on a course that God is shaking and taking down. We must course-correct and get back to a structure and design that we see in Acts and the Epistles. We must deconstruct. We must operate in the Spirit, with a Kingdom mentality and establish a Biblical structure.

Before we move further, allow me to explain and elaborate on "Type vs. Anti-type".

Throughout the earth there is a constant battle between God and satan, between righteousness and evil, between genuine and counterfeit. Because we generally hold to a philosophy of man being good and questioning the existence of both God and His counter type, we operate throughout life with a skewed perception of reality. Each person is doing what is right in their own sight in reference to God. It is our belief system which will direct and dictate our moral compass.

It is imperative that each person resolve the issue of the existence of both God and an enemy who seeks to take people captive. In fact, until we are liberated by the blood of Jesus, we are the

71

enemy's slaves according to Paul in Romans 6: 16 "Do you not know that to whatever you yield yourselves as slaves for obedience, you are slaves to what you obey." For a deeper understanding, I discuss the dynamic of spiritual slavery in my book, BondSlave.

Here are the Type-Anti-types of the church and Ekklesia.

The satanic acceleration

If you are not familiar with Baphomet, allow me to provide a new awareness.

In an article written in Hyperallergic by Billy Anania, dated September 16, 2020, he has two objectives: establish that Satan does not exist and that the people self-identifying as Satanists are good people. He is quoted as saying, "You can really learn about people's cultural baggage by seeing how they react to the Baphomet monument," Greaves told Hyperallergic. "It's interesting to think that this debate could merely be about what's offensive to some type of individual, and that there is nothing qualitatively different about the Baphomet statue, which is openly symbolic of pluralism, diversity, and non-binary identity." (The Satanic Temple does not believe in the existence of Satan nor does it worship the occult.)

It is confusing to me why someone would promote an ideology regarding a non-deity they do not believe exists. Even so, I choose to embrace the definition of satanic systems and its many deviances and cultist practices.

If there was ever a time when polarization is prevalent, it is today. And as ecclesia, those who are chosen and set apart and given a purpose as the governing body of His kingdom, we need to make a choice. Elijah the prophet understood the issue and confronted his culture. Here is what he said to Ahab: "Send and gather to me all Israelites at Mount Carmel, together with the 450 prophets of Baal and the 400 prophets of Asherah who eat at Jezebel's table." So, Ahab (the king of Israel) did as he requested and sent word to all the children of Israel and gathered the (false) prophets to Mount Carmel.

Notice that Ahab was facing such a bad situation that the false prophets of Asherah had infiltrated his home. His wife, Jezebel, was feeding them and hosting them at his table!

The question Elijah posed to Israel is the same question facing us today. "How long will you waver between two opinions? If Adonai is God, follow Him, but if Baal is, follow him."

We, the Christians in the USA, have accommodated the Baal and Luciferians into our homes and lives. We are oblivious to the level of luciferin worship by Hollywood, their artists, professional athletes, musical artists, masonic temples, corporations, and churches. We are oblivious to the purveyance of those who are practicing Wiccans, witches, the use of horoscopes, séances, psychic lines, mediums, satanic temples, satanic rituals, sacrifices, spells, and incantations, which are offered worldwide every day.

Once you see the symbolism, the secret handshakes, the gestures, the color schemes, and the numerological systems, you cannot but see what has been right in front of you all along. There is an increased level of overt, in-your-face, arrogant disregard for God's laws and holiness. The God-given boundaries have been exceeded and God has given the perverse *"over in the evil desires of their hearts to impurity,...given them up to shameful passions, and given them over to a depraved mind to do what is not fitting (Romans 1:24-28)."* He certainly is a counterfeiter, a schemer, and a master illusionist.

If you cannot figure out where the battle is coming from, pick one of the groups above and do a little research. We have been naïve and ignorant for too long. I know that in my childhood, we thought it was all innocent. But the foundation was being laid. Drugs were being introduced and eastern philosophies piggy-backed on the hard rock rhythms being produced.

There was a move of God in the Jesus People movement. We were losing the battle, though that was just one front. The battle was elevated for the heart and the mind. Marijuana was just the gateway to harder drugs. The sexual revolution was birthed then too. This era was mild compared to the escalation of sexual perversion it birthed. Pornography was just beginning to lure its captives. Addictions to new persuasions and variants arose and became normal and publicly acceptable.

I am purposely avoiding being descriptive because I hope to draw a female audience too. Biblically, we are not to speak about what is done in darkness, but we are told to "expose them."

"Take no part in the fruitless deeds of darkness, but rather expose them—for it is disgraceful even to mention the things that are done by them in secret (Ephesians 5:11-12)."

If you do not think the plans are intentional arrows against the family, against marriage, against children, please wake up.

"The gay agenda is here!"

The San Francisco Gay Men's Chorus Brags 'We're Coming for Your Children' in a new song, with lyrics that speak for themselves:

WE'LL CONVERT YOUR CHILDREN, HAPPENS BIT BY BIT, QUIETLY AND SUBTLELY [sic] AND YOU WILL BARELY NOTICE IT…

WE'LL CONVERT YOUR CHILDREN, REACHING ONE AND ALL. THERE'S REALLY NO ESCAPING IT 'CAUSE EVEN GRANDMA LIKES RUPAUL. AND THE WORLD'S GETTING KINDER. GEN Z'S GAYER THAN GRINDR…

WE'RE COMING FOR THEM WE'RE COMING FOR YOUR CHILDREN WE'RE COMING FOR THEM WE'RE COMING FOR THEM WE'RE COMING FOR YOUR CHILDREN FOR YOUR CHILDREN…

How much more overt does it have to get for you to engage in the battle for your children?

Speaking of children, I encourage you to look at Walt Disney. I know he became a household name for safe movies and family entertainment. But in retrospect, he was not what he appeared to be. His movies had a targeted audience—your children. The subliminal messages, the eventual path of many of their stars to the underground involvements. Please, do some research. There are so many ties and connections in this cesspool that are getting exposed. There are many interconnected parts globally.

While you are at it, the church is not exempt either. I will allow you to do your own research. Churches, for the most part, have been quiet and submissive during the lockdown. I understand the 501(c)(3) process as I started a nonprofit organization back in a 2014 filing with the IRS. There are a couple of questions that are targeted to see if the organization filing is or has any political leanings or involvements. Depending on how you answer these questions, you are granted or denied 501(c)(3) status.

The nonprofit application started in 1954 and became known as the Johnson Amendment.

From Wikipedia: *"The Johnson Amendment is a provision in the U.S. tax code, since 1954, that prohibits all 501c non-profit organizations from endorsing or opposing political candidates. Section 501(c) organizations are the most common type of nonprofit organization in the United States, ranging from charitable foundations to universities and churches. The amendment is named after the then-Senator Lyndon B. Johnson of Texas, who introduced it in a preliminary draft of the law in July 1954. Essentially, the Johnson Amendment was a compromise between the Federal Government and the church, allowing tax-exempt status in exchange for silence on anything politically."*

In David Fiorazo's article entitled "The Johnson Amendment and the Agenda to Silence Christians," he makes this comment [https://davidfiorazo.com/2015/05/the-johnson-amendment-and-the-agenda-to-silence-christians/]:

"We did not get here overnight. Attacks on religious freedoms and on the speech of Christians in America did not just appear in the last several years. The attempted muzzling of Christian churches and religious groups has gradually increased since a pivotal law was passed by a shrewd politician to intimidate people of faith. The repercussions have been devastating. The 1954 Johnson Amendment passed by Congress stated that non-profits (i.e. Christian churches and organizations) could not speak in favor of any political candidate. Was this even constitutional? Johnson knew how to use the political process to silence his enemies. The new amendment not only protected him from the conservative nonprofit groups opposing him, but many pastors stopped speaking about any issue from the pulpit that might be deemed political either out of ignorance of the new law or out of fear. By this self-censoring, the church has chosen to ignore open immorality in culture and government while at the same time neglecting to call attention to those political leaders who do strive to live according to Christian morals and values."

The Church has, for the most part, been effectively "muzzled" ever since. Pastors are not willing to risk losing their 501(c)(3) status. In losing their voice, they also disengaged from the political process and slowly embraced the narrative of the world separating church and state. The problem is, the Johnson Amendment did not silence the church's antagonists. Their voice got stronger and dominant.

"A rattlesnake bit one of my sheep in the face about a week ago. It is the deadliest snake that lives around here. The sheep's face swelled up and hurt her terribly.

But the old rattlesnake didn't know the kind of blood that flows through the sheep. Anti-venom is most often made from sheep's blood. The sheep swelled for about 2 days but the blood of the lamb destroyed the venom of the serpent.

I was worried but the sheep didn't care. She kept on eating, kept on drinking, and kept on climbing because she knew she was alright.

Often, the serpents of this life will reach out and bite us. They inject their poison into us but they cannot overcome the Blood of the Lamb of God that washes away the sin of the world and the sting of death. Don't worry about the serpent or his bite; just make sure that the Lamb's Blood is flowing through your veins."

Author Unknown

The church has been bitten by a snake. How many of our churches and pastors believe in the separation of church and state? How many preach that they are solely supported by your tithes, offerings, and gifts?

How many of you would be surprised to know that your church applied for and received money from the federally funded PPP loan program? If you do not believe me, here is a link to the Federal site: https://www.federalpay.org/paycheck-protection-program

Since this program is federally funded, the information is public knowledge. I was not shocked to find that many of the large denominational churches received money they do not have to pay back during the lockdown. What church or pastor is going to speak against the hand that feeds it? You can check anywhere in the United States, any state, city, or by name. Just select the appropriate fields and you will find that many of our large mega-churches applied for and received PPP money.

I hope this exercise serves to underscore how compromised our churches are today. I encourage you to review your church's budgets and see where the lion's share of the monies is delegated. You will be able to see a church's priority by tracing the categories to which monies are paid. I did a lot of networking over the past seven years of presiding over The Widows Project. I solicited budgetary support from churches and pastors. Over the course of those seven years, we had two churches that donated to The Widows Project. Each was a one-time gift and not annual, residual support donations. I sat at the table and watched other church plants, other non-profits that supported the local Gospel Mission, Young Life, Teen Pregnancy Center, Single Mothers, Adoption programs, etc., to receive support.

I get that budgets only go so far, but these women are our mothers and grandmothers. Look at the scriptures! Where are widows in the scripture in priority of care? It was a revelation not only that the church in general did not see the widow, but they chose not to see. I would get the proverbial pat on the back and the gratuitous "you are doing a magnificent work," but little engagement and minimal support.

I would have people find us and they would express their interest to meet up and have a conversation. Then they would ask about the compensation and I would smile at them and say, "The reward is service. Even I am a volunteer. I have self-funded to this point." They usually graciously end the conversation. Then they would walk away, never to be heard from again.

I would be happy to be proven wrong, but, to me, the lack of engagement by the church at large is an indication of the true state of the church. The local church follows the lead of the senior pastor. If the pastor doesn't see the need, neither will the sheep. Widows, orphans, prisoners, addiction support groups, and the homeless do not pay the bills. They are not income generators. These groups require resources; they are a drain and not a source of financial gain or return.

However, God does promise to bless those who care for the widow and orphan.

Deuteronomy 14:29: *"Then the Levite, because he has no portion or inheritance with you, along with the outsider, the orphan, and the widow within your gates will come and eat and be satisfied so that ADONAI your God may bless you in all the work of your hand that you do."*

It is a question of obedience to God's value system. These are whom He has come to seek and save. These are the ones that God speaks of in Isaiah 58 and Matthew 25:31-46. Are we willing to be obedient and avoid God's judgment or are we willing to risk His wrath? Is it possible that God is shaking the church today because it has strayed from His objectives? We get caught up in theological arguments rather than meeting the needs of depraved and starving mankind.

How can we get back to the model of the new community of faith that Peter, Paul, Jacob, John the revelator, Timothy, and Silas helped to build? We are told "no one was in want."

How do we walk in step with the Holy Spirit and experience an outpouring of the Holy Spirit and see 3,000 saved and more added daily? How do we change and establish a new culture?

I did a little research and couldn't find a book I read back in the late '70s or early '80s, titled New Wine, Old Wineskins (I believe this to be the title). All I can recall is the radical idea by the author, who suggested that churches should sell their buildings, rent offices, and invest the money they save and procure through the sale into ministries.

I would go a step further and suggest that they should take the lead of the Holy Spirit and find their priorities in Isaiah 58 and Matthew 25:31-46. When I searched the scriptures to find God's heart, I read these scriptures and James (Jacob) 1:27 to discover who has God's heart. He loves the world according to John 3:16, but He has an affinity toward some specific people groups: the poor, the stranger, the prisoner, the orphan, and the widow. After I determined God's heart, I then began to search the internet to see where care was lacking or non-existent. I then allowed the scriptures, which are inspired by the Holy Spirit, to be my guide.

Years ago, I read a study conducted by a man named Henry T. Blackaby, titled "Experiencing God." His main premise was to watch for God, see where He is moving, and then join Him. Not bad advice.

The home movement of the Ekklesia is where the next move of God is coming upon. It is the second move of the Holy Spirit.

> *Dean Briggs masterfully poses this question in his book* *Ekklesia Rising, "unless you get the question right, the* *answer will always be wrong." His question is, (fill in the* *blank): "Upon this rock I will build My _____?" He* *continues, "Did Jesus promise to build a church or an* *ekklesia? That is the question. The Great Commission was* *never given to a kuriakon or a church. It doesn't have the* *tools, nor the DNA. No, the mission of Christ uniquely* *requires the ekklesia to rise (pg. 121)."*

CHAPTER 7

THE CHARACTER OF THE ENEMY: TYPE VS. ANTI-TYPE CLUE: WATCH FOR THE ENEMY'S INVOLVEMENT IN EVERY AREA OF LIFE, ESPECIALLY THE FAMILY AND CHURCH.

Satan needs to destroy America. It's his grand prize. The need consumes him. He fantasizes about it. He pursues the destruction of the US with extreme prejudice and unrelenting patience.

Why do you need to know about Satan's passion to destroy America? Without this insight, you cannot muster the necessary urgency to obey God. You must know what is at stake to be willing to pay the price.

America is a firewall that prevents the one event Satan craves most: global anarchy.

Anarchy is the only thing that will make the world embrace the devil's worldwide dictatorship.

This is why the most important goal of evil is chaos.

Keep your eyes on Jesus and keep contending, worshipping, resting, praising, and declaring! God is on His Throne and the puny little Satan will not have his way!! ~MMM Team (Facebook post by Mario Murillo Ministry)

"You must become who He (Christ) says you are. You have been summoned to deliberate, legislate, and exert the will of God against demonic systems, injustice, and false ideologies. Ekklesia, remember who you are!" Dean Briggs, Ekklesia Rising pg. 210.

"God created humankind in His image; in the image of God He created him; male and female He created them." Genesis 1: 27

Image is everything and God tells us who we are, made and "created in His image." There are many areas through which Satan is attacking mankind, especially when it comes to redefining who man and woman are. He is forcibly taking hostage the global and cultural narrative defining our gender and sexual identities. The indoctrination is beginning at younger and younger ages. Many of our churches and pastors are embracing Satan's narrative rather than proclaiming the biblical declaration given by God about who we are.

One of my favorite lines from the 1995 movie "The Usual Suspects" is the line by Kevin Spacey's character Roger Kint (aka, Verbal), when he says,

> CLUE: *"The greatest trick the devil ever pulled was convincing the world he didn't exist."*

The line tells us something about the character of Satan, the devil. He is a deceiver, a liar, a master schemer, counterfeiter, who seeks to "steal, kill, and destroy (NASB)" or "steal, slaughter, and destroy (TLV)," according to John 10:10.

I want to share some observations I made of the three recordings of the "Temptation passages" in the gospels. What influence has the demonic realm played in history? Do we go back to the Old Testament (OT) or begin with the New Testament (NT)? If we use the NT, do we begin with the Temptation of Jesus in the wilderness? I wonder if we do a disservice to the scripture if we treat this account as a one-off? Notice that at the conclusion of the wilderness encounter between Jesus and Satan:

- Mark 1:12-13 mentions the event and timing but no details.
- Matthew 4:1-11 details the account and three temptations, Jesus commanding Satan to leave, while Luke makes an interesting claim.
- Luke 4:1-14 .... He (Jesus) now filled with the Ruach ha-Kodesh, returned from the Jordan. He was led by the Ruach in the wilderness for forty days, being tested by the devil. Verse 13: "And when the devil had completed every test, *he departed from Him until another occasion."*
- The devil was not through with Jesus. We see Jesus encountering demons, but we do not have scriptural evidence of further direct encounters with Satan till Passion Week.

85

- In Luke 22: 3, we are told that "Satan entered into Judah" (Judas), and later in vs. 31, Jesus tells Simon Peter that "Satan has demanded to sift you like wheat".

- By contrast, we see that Judah, grieved by his actions, went back to the ruling kohanim, tossed the thirty pieces of silver into the Temple sanctuary, and "he went out and hanged himself" Matt. 27:5.

- Luke, by contrast, says that Judas used the reward to purchase a field and, "falling headfirst, he burst open in the middle and his intestines splattered out".

- Matthew calls the 30 pieces of silver "blood money" and says that the priests took the money and bought a field for the burial of foreigners.

- If Judas were as distraught as the scriptures portray, for him to be of the mind to purchase a property for the purpose of hanging himself would take time. I wonder if the kohanim purchased the property where Judas hung himself.

- Regardless, the statement, "another occasion" or "opportune time", lends itself to an interpretation of future intervention by Satan. I contend that Satan has always sought out opportune times to wreak havoc, kill, steal, take hostage, destroy, scheme, counterfeit, and sabotage what God has created and declared. Primary among his targets are family (man/woman/children), marriage, and worship.

CHAPTER 8

LIFESTYLE CHANGES, CULTURAL SHIFT

> CLUE: How many times do we see
> "fear" mentioned in the bible?
>
> Answer: Over 500 times in the KJV

"I've learned that possibly the greatest detractor from high performance is fear: fear that you are not prepared, fear that you are in over your head, fear that you are not worthy, and ultimately, fear of failure. If you can eliminate that fear—not through arrogance or just wishing difficulties away, but through hard work and preparation—you will put yourself in an incredibly powerful position to take on the challenges you face." ~ Pete Carroll

"For as he thinks within himself, so is he." Proverbs 23:7a

In 2010, the Seattle Seahawks NFL franchise hired Pete Carroll as the head coach and executive vice president of the organization. When they hired Pete, he not only changed the personnel and coaching staff, but he also changed the narrative and culture of the team.

He knew that if the team was going to become a successful winning team, he needed to change their identity and the way they as an organization and team see themselves. He immediately instituted a "compete" first attitude. No one had a guaranteed position as a player. Everyone knew they could compete and win a position on the team.

If Pete and general manager, John Schneider, felt they could better the team at a certain position, they did it. They brought in many players for tryouts the first two years. They drafted differently than other teams. They had a specific prototype of physicality and speed, and within a couple of years, they were competing, winning, and crowned as Super Bowl Champions.

As the community of faith, we also need to change our mindset from the religious past to a new attitude, a new identity, and a new lifestyle. We do not realize that we have been indoctrinated and encultured by the world system we live in.

Here are a few proposed changes we need to make as Ekklesia. (These proposals are not necessarily in the order of priority).

1. Transition to a "New Identity" by using "Ekklesia" and leaving the word "church" behind.

Identity is important. Language is important too. The words we use mold and shape us. Many of us love to quote Romans 8:28 and for good reason, "we love God."

How many of us know the verse following twenty-eight? Paul talks about us *"being conformed to the image of His Son."* This is an integral part of the process of becoming Jesus bearers, by being "conformed" to the "image" of Jesus. Jesus is the one who told us we are Ekklesia.

When we fully embrace our image, which Jesus has given us, we are agreeing and being who He told us we are. For centuries, pastors have told us that both church and Ekklesia are synonymous. They are not even close to the same. One is static and inanimate. The other is alive and mobile. One breathes and speaks. The other is silent and does not breathe.

I know this is difficult. You are conflicted by the memories of the music, preaching, fellowship, and potlucks—of youth camp, revival meetings, and mission efforts. But how true to the biblical text of Matthew 16:18 have we been? How much like Matthew 25:31-46 have we been? How many times have you heard Isaiah 58 preached? Are you satisfied by giving up a meal and calling it a fast? Our preaching has gotten soft and as a result, so are we.

Did you know that God is a hater? We have allowed the world to give us the narrative about who God is! Did you know that God is only 'love?" That is what the world says, and our pastors have swallowed it hook, line, and sinker! My bible tells me that God hates.... (Wait for it!) ...do you know? ... sin—"haughty eyes, lying tongue, hands that shed innocent blood, a heart that plots wicked schemes, feet that run to evil, a false witness who spouts lies, and one who stirs up strife among brothers (Proverbs 6:16-19)."

2. Transition to Celebrating the "New man!"

Many of us love to quote this familiar scripture too—2 Corinthians 5:17. You may not recognize the address, but you know it as this: "Therefore, if anyone is in Messiah, he is a new creation. The old things have passed away; behold, all things have become new."

My question is, why do we continue to celebrate the old man?

I think the enemy of our souls would much prefer we celebrate the old man and not be reminded of who we now belong to!

How many of you still celebrate your "birth" day? You know, the physical birth we all experienced. I propose that, from this day forth, we who have been "born again" should start celebrating the "new birthday!"

First Place Ministries is going to launch a page on our website where you can register your "new birth" day and we will send you a "new birth" celebration ecard every year as a reminder.

Here is a link to our homepage: www.firstplaceministries.com. From there, look for the "New birthday" celebration registry.

Why is this important? For you parents and grandparents, here is another way to testify of your faith in Jesus to your friends and, more importantly, your children, your grandchildren, and your spiritual family! Our Messianic family has festivals or holidays all through the year to help remind them of God's redemptive work. For most New Testament followers of Jesus, we could use another event or date to testify of our faith in Jesus and pass our faith heritage on to the next generation.

3. Embrace a "New Berean Lifestyle"

In Acts 17:11, Luke introduces us to a group of Jesus followers whose identity is described as ones who were "searching the Scriptures each day (daily) to see whether these things were true."

I have embraced a Berean lifestyle for well over 15 years and I have developed an inductive, journaling system for studying the Bible called the "Choose Life Journal."

Many of us have been enculturated to read a daily devotional. My challenge is to take your personal relationship with Jesus to another level. For you married men or women, would you prefer to read a devotional of someone else's thoughts about your spouse, or would you rather read their words about you or to you?

Jesus is described in the scripture as the "Bridegroom." Who is He the bridegroom of? Did you automatically say "the church"? Remember, "church" was a substitution for Ekklesia and Ekklesia is "people" — you and I who are born again of water and spirit. Why do we not have marriage in heaven (Matthew 22:30)?

Since Jesus is the "Bridegroom" (Matthew 9:15), then who is the bride (Revelation 19:6b-9)? Could it be that Israel who is covenanted with God could be married to Elohim, and the

Ekklesia and kedoshim are betrothed to Jesus? I know they are one, but could it be? Anyway, I invite you to embrace a Berean lifestyle and get into the word daily.

In his book, "Holy Fire," R.T. Kendall underscores the lifestyle battle we are in today.

"Satan will do everything he possibly can to lure you away from tasting the genuine power of the living God. I want to anticipate certain cautions you may face down the road. Whether your background is conservative evangelical, Reformed, charismatic, or Pentecostal, there are certain pitfalls you need to be aware of. In each of these streams, you need to be armed to withstand the pressures that come from a revengeful Satan who does not want you to grow in grace and knowledge of our Lord Jesus Christ. 'My people are destroyed for lack of knowledge' (Hos. 4:6). In this connection, I would mention (1) lack of knowledge of God's Word and (2) lack of knowledge of God's ways."

Dr. Kendall's prescription is twofold: read the Bible and Prayer. He says this about each: "The devil does not want you to read your Bible, much less spend a lot of time reading the Bible. How well do you know your Bible? To understand the Bible, you must be on good terms with the Holy Spirit. He wrote the Bible."

"All Scripture is inspired by God and useful for teaching, for reproof, for restoration, and for training in righteousness, so that the person belonging to God may be capable, fully equipped for every good deed. 2 Timothy 3:16-17

"For no prophecy was ever brought forth by human will; rather, people spoke from God as they were moved by the Ruach ha-Kodesh." 2 Peter 1:21.

He alone can open your mind to understand His Word. He underscores, *"You need a plan,"* and we have one for you at First Place Ministries.

Secondly, "the way you know someone's ways is by spending time with them. You show your esteem of a person by how much time you give to them. So, I will come right to the point: *How often do you pray? The devil does not want you to pray, much less spend a lot of time praying (pg. 2-3)."*

Dean Briggs agrees with the priority of prayer. *"Prayer is fundamental. It's the baseline. How can we be His house if we aren't characterized by a culture of prayer?"*

The two things I strongly encourage you to install as disciplines into your life daily are a systematic time in the Word of God and Prayer. I promise that the Holy Spirit will lead you into all truth and many new discoveries. He will empower your life. He promises: "But you will receive power when the Ruach ha-Kodesh has come upon you," power to "witness."

At First Place Ministries, we focus on the
Word and Contending Prayer daily!

We can help you establish a daily time in the word with our Choose Life Journal plan and our Contending Prayer Call via zoom.

Please subscribe at www.firstplaceministries.com/subscribe to receive our daily Choose Life Journal and to join us on our zoom call. We encourage you to grow and engage on the prayer call and by doing your own journal.

4. Discipleship is a mandate.

First Place Ministries strives to fulfill the Great Commission by "Discipling" the kedoshim, those who are born again, helping you to establish the disciplines of daily study in the Bible and Prayer. I have already discussed how to engage in our daily Choose Life Journaling program. There is another discipline that is a vital characteristic of those who desire to live a lifestyle of holiness unto Jesus.

The only request the disciples made of Jesus was to teach them to pray (Luke 11:1-4). Even having launched our Contending Prayer call on May 1st of 2021, I am still frequently asking the Holy Spirit to teach me to pray.

A new discovery I made a couple of months into our Prayer Call is found in Ephesians 6:18a: *"Pray in the Ruach on every occasion, with all kinds of prayers and requests."*

There are all kinds of contentions about praying in tongues or prayer language. You resolve it on your own, but I see this declaration by Paul to the Ephesians as a non-negotiable directive. I have determined how I can best comply with Paul's directive under the guidance of the Holy Spirit. In my understanding, this is a "do," not a point of argument or disagreement.

I love knowing that the Holy Spirit "intercedes for us with groans too deep for words." I love knowing that He (the Holy Spirit) "intercedes for the *kedoshim* according to the will of God."

Once again, I quote from Romans 8:26-27, two verses prior to vs. 28, which we all quote so regularly. I encourage you to know the whole word of God, which you only get by the discipline of study. Fall in love with your Bridegroom and study, and time with Him becomes automatic.

5. Decide on Intentional Fellowship & Worship

The early community of faith is characterized by intentional "fellowship...to breaking bread (from house to house), and to prayers (Acts 2:42)." During the lockdown, many of us felt the loss of personal, relational interaction—one to another. We discovered we could accomplish a lot of networking and business via a social media & video platform. But this did not replace human contact. There is a non-negotiable need for human-to-human contact. We need each other. Many have asked me, in the context of establishing Ekklesia groups, how we find each other. First Place Ministries wants to be at the forefront of helping the ekklesia find each other. If you would like to form an Ekklesia group or would like to find a group, please check out our new Ekklesia Find-a-Group Directory through this link: https://www.firstplaceministries.com/. You can find or register a group on this registry. Please list a contact email address, general area of residence (no addresses will be listed), and what type of group you are hosting (fundamental, evangelical, spirit-filled, messianic) so that like-minded people can find you. We desire to be an Ekklesia D3 (Distribution, Discipleship & Directory) epicenter.

6. Scrutinize your Holiday Celebrations

I can remember thinking it weird that a family I grew up with did not celebrate Christmas. They broke with the enculturated practice of the world and organized religion and instilled in their children their convictions about this non-holy, institutional holiday. I have just offended many. As if it were not bad enough that I picked on the not-so-sacred institution of the church, could I not leave Christmas alone? Well, if we are going to purge, let's do it right and not partially. When Joshua led the Hebrew children into the Promised Land, they were tasked with purging or eradicating everything from the land. They compromised and it cost them dearly for the rest of their lives.

My parents always saved Christmas Eve for the spiritual, biblical narrative of sharing the birth of Jesus from Luke 2:1-20. Dad read this passage and then we, many times, sang Christmas carols while he played the accordion. I have fond memories of those evenings, which were usually highlighted with cookies, nuts, and mom's homemade peanut brittle. I encourage you to consider establishing a family tradition with the spiritual significance of Christmas. Grandparents, it is a perfect opportunity to pass along your spiritual heritage and create an intimate spiritual experience.

Also, I want to mention concern for the engagement of our children in the unholy and seemingly innocent involvement in Octween. I am not using the cultural name, as it is anything but "hallow." I hope I have effectively established by this point in the book that satanic activity is anything but innocent and safe. Please establish ahead of time your family policy and how you

96

are going to educate your children about this culturally accepted event. Let us heed Paul's warning in Ephesians 5:11: *"Take no part in the fruitless deeds of darkness, but rather expose them."*

7. Consider Home or Private Schooling for your Children

Most recently, I completed a seven-year career with a local school district in Washington State as a school bus driver. I can say from firsthand experience that I would not want to have a child attending a public school today.

The things I saw posted in teachers' lounges and student conversations I overheard on the bus were concerning. Our children are bombarded, pressured, and indoctrinated into a world system that my age group did not have to face growing up.

We faced debates about evolution versus creationism and philosophies about drugs, psychedelics, and cultic mystical religions, but our children are faced with so much more. I have emphasized the importance of "image," and "image" is being hugely challenged, especially in gender identity and critical race theory. Faith-based schools or home-schooling is now necessary than ever before. I encourage parents to consider protecting their children by knowing the in- "formation" your children are receiving. I hope the Ekklesia movement can have a prominent influence on the education of children and adults. This is critically important. Your schooling system needs to support your values.

8. Healthcare and Health Insurance

My prayer is that someone who has the wherewithal to institute a faith-based movement in the Healthcare and Health Insurance industries can institute a major paradigm shift in both industries, which reflects biblical principles of people care. Most hospitals originated in or from the church or faith. But they, like our seminaries, have wandered from their roots. I pray that you will join me in the dismantling of the abortion industry. I hope you are aware of the evils that are being exposed about its underground workings.

9. Financial shift

One World currency and money systems are allegedly already in place. Again, if you are reading my book and have the wherewithal to launch a network of faith-based financial systems, I hope you will engage. I am not convinced that our financial systems have ever possessed integrity and where money is involved, it is naïve to think it could ever become such. We have been slaves of the system for centuries and to turn a world system around will be epic, miraculous, only something our Supreme ruler of heaven and earth can accomplish. Justice is His and will one day be accomplished.

10. Generosity

We have talked about the early faith communities' attitude and practice of generosity. They had apostles whom they trusted to distribute to those in need. We need anointed, spirit-filled people whom we trust to distribute the resources that are received. I am open for a dialogue with spirit-filled people who understand the system that needs to be put in place and administered. We have a model in Acts 6:1-7, when a dispute arose between two widow's groups. The fascinating part of this passage to me is that the apostles identified the problem, delegated the solution, and the problem is never mentioned again. The apostles continued in the work and calling they were given, and seven men full of the Holy Spirit were found and called into action to "serve." They were all spirit-filled volunteers as were the apostles. They didn't serve to make a living; they served as a lifestyle.

Allow me to add that everyone, no matter your financial position in life, rich or poor, on social security or abundantly wealthy, has something to be generous about. It is an attitude and not a ledger line. I want to share with you the story of a couple of people who have crossed my life's path and have blessed others with the abundance or abilities God has given them.

I met an elderly, grandmotherly type of woman while living in Southern California who loved to crochet. To my knowledge, she was not rich and certainly humble. She launched a baby blanket-making ministry. She would gift mothers whom she discovered were pregnant with a blanket made with love. They were colorful, unique, and always warmly received. She used what she had to bless others.

I was raised in a home that practiced the same generosity. My parents were not wealthy, but what we had—a large garden and several fruit trees — provided us opportunities to bless others with quality home-grown produce. I saw them give a lot of vegetables and fruits away. God always provided us with a garden that produced in abundance.

I hope that you found the above **Ten Lifestyle/Cultural Shift suggestions** helpful in making some needed changes in your thinking and your life. Our identity is critically important to who we are in and to Jesus. How can you be or become who you were designed to be if you do not know who you are? I pray that the spirit of confusion that has enslaved us for decades and centuries is broken and you are freed in Jesus' name. May you, today, begin a new and/or renewed walk with Jesus.

First Place Ministries is here to help you begin and continue your new journey with Jesus as His Ekklesia! Amen.

CHAPTER 9

CHECKMATE!

> *CLUE: In the game of chess, it is the king who is being pursued!*

Proverbs 20:2: "The terror of a king is like a lion's growl. Whoever provokes him endangers his life."

Isaiah 43:18-19a: "Do not remember former things, nor consider things of the past. Here I am, doing a new thing."

"He was sent to drain the swamp! To be a wrecking ball! To create, to be a caveat of chaos. To be a contradiction. So that the church would get in place to be the prophetic voice it was meant to be." Dr. Kynan Bridges on President Donald J. Trump.

While I disagree with the use of the word "church," Dr. Bridges is correct. Trump was and is a catalyst for the Ekklesia to arise and be the prophetic voice it was meant to be!

I would like to offer you a prophetic quote from the late world-renowned prophet, Kim Clement, given on April 4, 2008 in Seattle, Washington:

"And they shall say, 'but there is a second President. How can we have two presidents?' 'An unusual thing, isn't it?' says the Spirit of the Lord. Why would it be that one with a double mind would stand up and face the people? No, they shall say, 'We have two presidents. What do we do now?'" ~**Kim Clement**

[Here's the link to the full video: https://youtu.be/W3hPnxp6HlQ]

I had the pleasure of hearing Kim Clement at his Renton, Washington meeting around 2005. I did not understand what I was hearing; it was all foreign to me. Nonetheless, this encounter was a God-ordained appointment. Along with the dream I referenced in this book, this was the genesis of God transitioning me from the religious idols, icons, and structures in my life.

Is it too late? We do not know when Jesus will return. From the time of Paul (Philippians 3:20, 1 Thessalonians 4:13-18; Jacob; i.e. James 5:8 and John the Revelator 1:3b, 22:10, 20), we know they all believed Jesus' return was imminent and soon. Regardless, we must be prepared and band together. The church, universal and institutional, has forsaken Yahweh and He is doing a new thing in new wineskins. For those who love God and desire to keep His commandments, welcome home!

You may have felt abandoned by the church, but you were not abandoned by Jesus. He told us before His ascension into heaven: "remember, I am with you always, even to the end of the age (Matthew 28:20b) and "For God Himself has said, I will never leave you or forsake you, so that with confidence we say, 'The Lord is my helper; I will not fear. What will man do to me?" (Hebrews 13:5b-6)

We must organize and coordinate this move of God among His Ekklesia. First Place Ministries stands ready to assist by locating each other so that we can be who Jesus declared in Matthew 16:18, *"Upon this rock I will build My Community (Ekklesia); and the gates of Sheol will not overpower it. I will give you the keys of the kingdom of heaven."*

We must be intentional to seek fellowship and face-to-face worship.

We must share the gospel, baptize, and disciple the newly born again.

We must study the word like the Bereans and be a community of prayers.

We must look anxiously for Jesus' return.

We must share communion together to remember His death till He returns.

We must be a generous, giving community.

We can never return to the garden. Man was ushered (escorted) out of the garden and angel guardians were posted to prevent our return. However, there is nothing to prevent us from returning to the first-century model of the new community of faith. They did a fabulous job without planes, trains, automobiles, mobile phones, and the internet.

We will face the same problems and scrutiny of the church. Expect it. *We will be labeled as illegitimate, but the Spirit will decide.* Those who are His have the Spirits seal of approval according to Ephesians 1:13-14: *"After you heard the message of truth—the Good News of your salvation—and when you put your trust in Him, you were sealed with the promised Ruach ha-Kodesh. He is the guarantee of our inheritance, until the redemption of His possession—to His glorious praise!"*

CHAPTER 10

LEGITIMACY OF HOME-BASED WORSHIP VS. LEGITIMACY OF THE CHURCH

"Church has become so ingrained in our religious and secular cultures that the mere suggestion that this word is wrong sends shivers down denominational spines." Tim Kurtz, pg. 146, Leaving Church, Becoming Ekklesia.

"Upon this rock I will build My Ekklesia; and the gates of Sheol will not overpower it." Matthew 16:18 TLV.

CLUE: Remember Matthew 16:18

I t seems that the moment the institutional, denominational church wants to flex its muscles the issue of legitimacy arises. Sure, it does not have the structure of a church because it is not a church. It is simple in form and structure. What Jesus declared simple in structure, man has made complex. Huge budgets, large complexes, impersonal, controlling, structured worship, entertainment, must be a great speaker, degree-focused rather than spirit-controlled, always appeals for money, and servicing large debt. Is this what Jesus had in mind?

I have been in the church all my life. So, I have seen the church from the pew, the pulpit, from the congregation, and as a pastor. I have journeyed from the evangelical ranks to the charismatic and on to the home-based movement. From denominationalism to non-denominationalism, and on to a kingdom lifestyle. I was raised on the King James Bible, schooled with the New American Standard Bible, and transitioned to the Tree of Life Version Bible a few years ago.

I have survived through church splits and many Senior Pastoral changes. I have experienced and witnessed moral failures. I have seen and experienced the church "shoot their wounded." I have worked for and founded a nonprofit ministry. I have seen firsthand how the church treats the parachurch world.

I have lived through a change of philosophy of the church every decade: from every church had to have a Sunday school, then a youth program, then a children's program, then a bus ministry, then a choir transitioned to a worship team. We must have a mission's program and a building campaign, and revival services along with a two-week Bible school in the summer and youth camp along with family camp. Keep the people busy and occupied and hopefully we slip in some actual worship, prayer, and Bible study. Perhaps, some of the funds will get to the people who need the help!

What does God want?

If we look at the scriptures, which give us a picture and form to home-based worship, we see they were *"devoting themselves to the teaching of the emissaries and to fellowship, to breaking bread and to prayers.* Fear lay upon every soul, and *many wonders and signs were happening through the emissaries. And all who believed were together, having everything in common.* They began *selling their property and possessions and sharing them with all, including anyone who had need.* Day by day, they continued with *one mind*, spending *time at the Temple* and *breaking bread from house to house.* They were *sharing meals with gladness and sincerity of heart, praising God, and having favor with all the people.* And *every day, the Lord was adding to their numbers those being saved" (Acts 2:42-47 TLV).*

CLUE: We begin with Simplicity!

There is so much to unpack here, but let us begin with simplicity. I see informality, intimacy, and being personal all over this passage. The emissaries or apostles were devoted to teaching in informal settings from house to house. The new converts were being transitioned from the formal to the informal, from structured (Temple) to the personal house to house.

This was a family setting for a new spiritual family in Jesus. Jesus was prophetically announcing a new kingdom and that a new family is approaching: "Here are My mother and My brothers! For whoever does the will of God, he is My brother and sister and mother (Mark 3:33-35 & Matthew 12:48-50)." He knew a new advent; a new spiritual family was about to be established. Here is the insider information. Are you listening?

There is a tendency to overlook the next sentence, *"__Fear lay upon every soul.__"* Sounds much like today. They were afraid of government oppression, too.

Roman oppression was great against the early faith community. The apostles had just witnessed Jesus' death, burial, resurrection, and ascension. They had received forty days of instruction before His ascension and now fifty days in, they and 120 others were together in an upper room about to receive the Holy Spirit, the most dynamic moment in Jesus' followers' lives. The inaugural sending and giving of the Ruach ha-Kodesh, the Holy Spirit.

One of the fallacies of the Church is to clone pastors and congregants and know what you know from being told what scripture says. There is not enough self-study and originality. I say that based on years of sermons and self-discovery in scripture.

In a recent study of the Gospel of Luke, I discovered that the word "Hosanna" in English is from the Hebrew word "Hoshia-na," meaning "save now." All I have heard my entire life is that "Hoshia-na" was the cry of the people as Jesus entered Jerusalem triumphantly. The cheers were those of celebration and rejoicing.

However, if we take the meaning of "Hoshia-na" literally, I contend that the shouts were pleas of "save us now," we are desperate to be liberated from tyranny and oppression. That paints a whole different picture of Jesus' triumphant entry. The people demanded physical freedom and Jesus brought spiritual deliverance from this world.

Have we reached the point where we are ready, desperate enough to cry out to Jesus, "Hoshia-na," save us now? I believe that many of us are crying in desperation and many more will be joining us in that cry in the coming months.

CLUE: *We add the Divine.*

Ever wonder why we do not see the "wonders and signs" that the early community of faith witnessed? No, I do not believe it was solely due to the Apostles or emissaries. No doubt they were anointed and now spirit-filled. However, we are told by Jesus through the writings of Mark that *"These signs will accompany those who believe: in My name they will drive out demons, they will speak new languages; they will handle snakes (I hate snakes); and if they drink anything deadly, it will not harm them; they will lay hands on the sick, and they will get well." (Mark 16:17-18 TLV).*

I believe that these words spoken by Jesus were meant for us today! These signs will accompany the ecclesia today. Imagine the Divine manifesting in the lives of Jesus' followers in signs and wonders. We will see breakthrough in signs and wonders very soon in the lives of the ecclesia and not the church.

Many prophets and pastors are saying that there is a move of God on the horizon. Jehovah God is going to do a new work. I believe that statement to be absolutely true.

However, according to Luke 5:36-39...
CLUE: this new move of God *will not be in*
the church, but in the Ekklesia.

Now he was also telling them a parable.

"No one tears a patch from a new garment to use it on an old garment. Otherwise, he will rip the new, and the patch from the new will not match the old.

And no one puts new wine into old wineskins. Otherwise, the new wine will burst the skins; it will be spilled out and the skins will be destroyed.

But new wine must be put into fresh wineskins.

No man who drinks old wine wants new because he says, '**The old is fine**.'

These are the words of Jesus.

CLUE: Do we want new wine or old wine?

We define wineskin as a vessel that contains the wine. Jesus establishes that one never puts new wine into old wineskins as they will rupture or burst. New wine requires new wineskins. Can we determine that the church is a form of wineskin? It is an illegitimate form, but none the less a form of wineskin. Luke quotes Jesus making an absolutely fascinating statement at the conclusion of the parable (which none of the other gospel writers mention): "No man who drinks old wine wants new, because He says, "The old wine is fine."

110

Where have we heard this before? There used to be a popular old gospel tune with lyrics that said, "It was good enough for …., then it's good enough for me." Unfortunately, many of us stay in this same mentality and settle for the old wine. Those who do will miss the miracles and wonders Jesus has assigned for these times. I pray that we see apostles, prophets, pastors, and evangelists arise in our day who drink of the new wine and form new home-based wineskins as reserves. Fill us Holy Spirit! Fill us now!

Clue: The Model is Distribution, Not Acquisition

One of the awakenings during this current journey in the word, the model of the early community in Acts 4: 34-35, is right before us in plain sight. It says that the people (the kedoshim, the saints, and the followers of Jesus via the disciples), "for all who were owners of lands or houses would sell them, bring the proceeds, and set them at the feet of the emissaries. *And the proceeds were distributed according to the need each one had.*"

I might have missed something here, so let's go back and review what we just read. It says that the people who were land and homeowners voluntarily (it was not mandated by Jesus or the government) sold their property and brought the proceeds to the apostles, laid the proceeds at their feet, and the proceeds were kept and put into the bank to build their assets to build a bigger building. *NO?* Oh, it was given so that the pastor could buy a bigger house. *NO?* Oh, the proceeds were given for the purpose of buying a jet plane for the pastor to fly around the globe to *make converts. No?* Hmmmm, what did I miss? It says the proceeds were to be *"distributed"!*

The early community of faith structure was that of being a "distribution center," not an acquisition center. Our pastors have made the Church a depository for paying staff, paying a mortgage, maintaining a building, building equity, buying vans, providing programs, building a large savings account, and the list goes on.

Those with the need will always continue in need if we continue with this model. The new faith community claimed, *"No one among them was in need."* How can they make that claim and the Church has never been able to make that claim? Because the Church is focused inward; it takes care of itself first!

How many sermons have you heard on tithing and giving? How many of you grasp that the tithing concept is a carry-over from the law in the Old Testament? How much does Jesus want from us? I see from Matthew 22:37 that He wants *"all"* our heart, mind, and soul. Is he satisfied with ten percent? What does He deserve? We can do ten percent; we can do twenty percent and feel satisfied. But what does Jesus require? Can you say you love Jesus with any less than 100%?

Man will never do more than he needs to unless He is compelled by his love for an all-sufficient Savior.

Easier to remember. Not easier to accomplish!

What did Jesus do by giving us a New Covenant? He simplified His Covenant with us. He made it easier to remember! He did not make it easier to accomplish.

If you take a closer look at the Ten Commandments found in Exodus 20, you will find that all the laws were based on two things: your relationship with God and your relationship with man. Jesus followed the same model given by Yahweh to Moses on Mount Sinai.

CLUE: Jesus did not require any less; He required it all.

"You shall love Adonai your God with *all* your heart, and with *all* your soul, and with *all* your mind."

In Malachi 3: 7-10, we hear these words. *"From the days of your ancestors, you have turned aside from My statutes, and have not kept them. Return to Me, and I will return to you," says* ADONAI-Tzva'ot. *Yet you say: "How should we return?"*

"Will a man rob God? For you are robbing Me!" But you say: "How have we robbed You?" "In the tithe and the offering. You have been cursed with the curse, yet you keep robbing Me—the whole nation!

Bring the whole tithe into the storehouse. Then there will be food in My House. Now test Me in this"—says ADONAI-Tzva'ot—*"if I will not open for you the windows of heaven, and pour out blessing for you until no one is without enough.*

If God will charge the Hebrew nation with "robbing" Him, what will He say to New Testament followers who are to give it all to Him?

I am wrestling with these same concepts. When I look at what I have, is it mine or is it His? Isn't it easier to give other people's money away? If we agree with God that it all belongs to Him, won't it be easier to give it back to Him for distribution? Do we trust the Church to be distributors and not acquisitionists? Do we trust non-profits to be the same? Do we see ourselves as managers rather than owners and possessors?

Here is another weakness in the Church model.

CLUE: Did the Great Commission tell us to "teach" or to "disciple"?

Every Pastor I know has preached the Great Commission, appropriately so. The obstacle is, again, with the word "church" and identification with a building that is static. The building cannot fulfill the commission as it cannot "go!" The people can, but will they? Not if they feel they do not see the commission as specifically given to them. The mindset is, "the mandate" was not specifically given to me. Therefore, it does not apply to me.

Too much of the mindset is, "this is the pastor's job." This is what he is getting paid to do. I can hear the objections. We have people who do evangelism or missionary work. That is not the point. What percentage of the congregation participates? It is only a small percentage that participates because the others do not own the commission. Is the commission given to every follower of

Jesus? Is the Great Commission not owned by every follower because of the institutional model of ownership? Are we going in Jesus' name or the name of our church or denomination?

> *CLUE: Going does not require travel,*
> *but it does require "going"*

I might add that the word "Go" requires movement. We can "go" to our own community. Going does not require travel. I have observed plenty of churches that "go" overseas and will not go to their own community or neighbor. Thousands will be spent on international travel, but they will not go to their own Jerusalem. The Great Commission tells us where to start. Perhaps, we should not go to the next step in the Commission until we have succeeded in going to our Jerusalem. Many of our communities could use the monies we have invested in going overseas, right at home. It is not that we need not be concerned about the $2/3^{rd}$ world poor countries, but we need to be self-righteous about what we are doing overseas, and oblivious to our neglect of the needs at home.

Another observation about the church model. We do not embrace ownership of the Great Commission nor do we take ownership of discipleship! I have shared why I transitioned from the King James Bible to New American Standard, and now to the Tree of Life Version. Many translations that came after the KJV are translations using the KJV as their foundation. We know from scripture that our model is only as good as the foundation we use.

I just recently discovered another important translation difference. In the Great Commission (Matthew 28:19-20), in the KJV, we read: "Go ye therefore, and teach all nations." In the TLV, we read, "Go therefore and *make disciples* of all nations." There is a vast difference between "teaching" and "making disciples." The church is guilty of making converts rather than making disciples. Are we going to be obedient to the word of Adonai or not? Which is the more accurate of translations? How can we use a translation that is not being accurate to the Hebrew, Greek, and Aramaic?

CLUE: *The same Holy Spirit who teaches your pastor, teaches you! There is only One Holy Spirit!*

Additionally, as followers of Jesus, we are lazy about spending time in the Word, the Bible. In my former church days, I selected my last church engagement because they were (according to their website) engaged in an inductive Bible Study system that I had just discovered.

So, I started attending worship services and built a relationship with the senior pastor and a couple of the associate pastoral staff. It became obvious to me that while the senior pastor typically preached about this system each year, imploring the congregants to engage in the daily Berean approach, few were faithfully following the system.

I attended this church for 15+ years and in the earlier years, I could tell that the senior pastor was engaged in this systematic process because he would elude in his sermons to something he had read in the word because of the scheduled reading.

At one point, about 5 years ago, because they knew I was doing the Bible study system, I was asked to lead a class, helping those who enrolled to develop a lifestyle of daily study. One couple and a friend of theirs are the only people who enrolled. Within a month, they and the friend dropped out. The disciplines of bible study are tough, and life got in the way. I get it. Unless we make an intentional decision to get into the word daily and set a specific time that we protect, it will not happen.

I will tell you: the process has been transformational for me and I believe you will experience the same thing. When it is you and the Holy Spirit, mano-a-mano, transformation will happen. You will not be disappointed!

We must take responsibility for our spiritual growth! Too many in the church do not assume personal responsibility. We go to worship, open our mouths, and say to the pastor, feed me! How many times do you hear, "I didn't get anything out of that sermon"? Or "my needs are not being met".

My question to you: "Why, at your age, are you still sitting in a spiritual highchair?" The bible is written in English. You know how to read! Pick up the spoon and the fork and feed yourself. It is a lie that you cannot understand the Bible. The same Holy Spirit who is teaching your pastor is the same Holy Spirit who will lead you into all truth according to John 14:26. If your pastor teaches you differently, he lies! The Holy Spirit is the One who has taught me and revealed to me the things I am exposing and sharing with you.

Right before Jesus declared to Peter, 'upon this rock I will build my Ekklesia," He told Peter, "flesh and blood did not reveal this to you; but My Father who is in heaven." Peter had just declared to Jesus' question, "Who do you say I am?" "You are the Messiah, the Son of the living God."

CHAPTER 11

MY SPIRITUAL JOURNEY

"In recent years, there has been a noticeable decline in 'church' attendance. Adherents to the institutional church usually lay the blame on those leaving. Some have suggested that this is the 'great falling away' or apostasy spoken of in the bible. I would suggest that it is neither. Why? Because many of those leaving the institutional church have not left their relationship with Jesus Christ. They only left a system that they believe has lost its authenticity. House, organic, and simple church groups became a plausible choice for those who recognized the continued need for fellowship with other believers. Let me quickly interject that most of these groups did not spring up because the people in them were dysfunctional. That has been a false label imposed upon them by some people in the institutional church system." Tim Kurtz pg. 147, Leaving Church, Becoming Ekklesia.

"Work out your salvation with fear and trembling. For the One working in you is God—both to will and to work for His good pleasure." Philippians 2:12b-13

"Hear now My words!" He (Adonai) said. "When there is a prophet of Adonai, I reveal Myself in a vision, I speak to him in a dream." Numbers 12:6

I was raised in an Evangelical Christian home. My parent's background was Lutheran and Friends/Quaker. In marriage, they landed in a Baptist Church, Trinity Baptist in Renton, Washington. It is a Southern Baptist denominational Church, which taught me a lot about the fundamentals of the faith in Christ, especially salvation. It was an Evangelical Church, so there was an altar call at every service, just in case someone in attendance might need to be saved. I made a profession of faith in Jesus at age 9 and I was diligent in seeking Him. I was quite indoctrinated. I knew what I thought I knew because of what I was told. It has been my journey in the past seventeen years, sitting at the feet of the Holy Spirit, to show me how much I did not know and still do not know.

We were religious in our attendance. We were there every time the door was open. Twice on Sunday (morning & evening), every Wednesday, all special events like weeklong revival services, Bible studies, and two weeklong Vacation Bible Schools. I attended Youth Camps and Youth Conventions.

My resolve was strong. I carried my Bible to school and the nickname Moses was given to me. In my High School era, we had Baccalaureate services a few days before graduation. It is a pseudo-religious ceremony in which the scripture is read and a few students are granted the honor of participating. I was selected and honored to read Matthew 6: 25-34. The schoolmate I walked in graduation with was selected to sing and she chose "Somewhere" (There's a place for us) from the musical Westside Story. She was a scholarship award winner headed to Baylor University (Wanda, I hope to see you in around His throne!).

But even with all the hours of sermons, Sunday School, and personal study, the conditioning of the church was not able to keep me strong from the bombardment of the conditioning of the world. I married and moved to Southern California to attend a private Christian Non-Denominational Liberal Arts University, Biola University, and returned to Washington State divorced and headed for a nearly, 30-year wilderness experience.

I had attended separate Billy Graham Crusades in Portland and Seattle at the Kingdome. It was the very first event in Seattle's now-demolished domed stadium. I knew I was born again, but something was missing. The power to live a Christ-like life was not present.

I had read Henry Blackaby's book "Experiencing God," which told you to look for God, and when you find where He is working, join Him. I listened to Walter Martin as the Bible Answer Man, and he waxed eloquently on the differences of Christianity to other religions and cults. I was indoctrinated in the Dispensational doctrine of Pre-Tribulation rapture, now called Cessationism.

I even read several books written by Francis Schaeffer. Then in the last 20 years, I came across an author, R.T. Kendall, who had a similar journey. By his own admission, he started his faith journey as a Nazarene, then joined the Southern Baptists and later became Spirit-filled or Charismatic. Unlike him though, it took me a lot longer. I always desired more of the Holy Spirit, not less. The disputes over the Holy Spirit to me are amazing yet confusing.

An Unfortunate Encounter

I remember my initial meeting of people who claimed charisma. It was a summer around 1970. I was at the Seattle Center on the World's Fairgrounds with a few of the youth from my church. (Remember, I knew what I thought I knew and in my mind that was settled. It had to be true! After all, it is what my parents embraced and confirmed. It was what my trusted pastor had told me. It was what the Church told me. It had to be true!)

We were approached by a group of Charisma-embracing youth. Somehow, we connected and were surrounded by other youth of faith. Unfortunately, arrogance rose within the other group, and someone had to ask the critical question, "Do you speak in tongues?" Immediately the walls go up and the conversation ended. The divide is fortified and the enemy has won. Oh, how I wish today they had approached us like Priscilla and Aquila approached Apollos in Acts 18: 24-28. We see no evidence of Apollos being offended. They approached him with compassion, grace, and loving-kindness. They did not invalidate his understanding of salvation, for he "had been instructed in the way of the Lord. With a fervent spirit, he was speaking and teaching accurately the facts about Yeshua while only being acquainted with the immersion of John." He knew about salvation in Jesus and Jesus only, but he did not know the Holy Spirit.

Religion and a religious spirit will always divide! It will always be arrogant. It will always be self-righteous. A kingdom spirit and a spirit led by the Holy Spirit will not be condemning or divisive. We don't have time for this type of pharisaical attitudes. I rebuke this religious spirit! This one incident set me back for most of 40 years. I wanted nothing to do with charismatic movement, but I still knew there was more to this journey with the Holy Spirit.

Two Transformational Encounters

I had two transformational encounters that I want to share with you. Both encounters happened around 2005.

A Divine Encounter

I was in a Christian bookstore and on the display was a book titled, The Divine Mentor by Wayne Cordiero. I was ready. The value of the book was to introduce me to a system of inductive Bible study that required you to journal and write out "daily" an application for the scripture assigned on that day. That simple act of meeting with the Holy Spirit daily and allowing Him to bring me into all truth has been transformational. I was not learning the thoughts of man, of the world, or a denomination. I was mano-a-mano with the Holy Spirit.

I have since created my inductive Bible system, called the **Choose Life Journal plan**. It is available at www.firstplaceministries.com as a free subscription.

A Divine Dream Encounter

The second encounter was a dream that I had, and I requested an interpretation from an Apostolic brother whose home fellowship I was attending. It has been around seventeen years since I had this dream, so the content, the details are not vividly clear, but the impact is still like yesterday. I remember seeing a wild beast running on a ridge, weaving in and out of columns and trees. The beast was dark, hairy, like a wolf but larger. As he passed the columns and trees, they fell over. After sharing the dream with my Apostolic brother, I gave him a few days to pray over it and get back to me. His interpretation was simple and direct. "God is tearing down the religious structure and idols in your life."

As I moved north in the Puget Sound area, I changed churches and knew that I was moving away from denominationalism and chose to attend a non-denominational Community Church that was Baptistic in doctrinal beliefs. I was there primarily for the softball program led by a fellow Biola Alumni. I was there for roughly five years and managed the number two team. Two things led me to leave this church.

The first was a spiritual gifts class. I thought it would be valuable to discover my gifting, so I attended the class hoping to receive some new enlightenment. I was not yet charismatic in my belief system, but I was dismayed by the absence of the spiritual manifestation gifts after taking the assessment. As I recall, even prophecy was missing.

Shortly after taking the class, I was in the foyer and spotted another softball coach talking with a man and walked over to them. I politely stood back, allowing them to finish their conversation. I wasn't eavesdropping, but it was impossible not to hear what they were discussing, and the conversation was not something that needed privacy. They were talking about a common friend who was in the hospital and was pronounced to have days to live. I remember interrupting and asking this coach if he had gone to pray over this man. He looked at me and said, *"He is past that point! It wouldn't do any good."*

I don't care which side of the fence you are on; I have always wanted more of the Holy Spirit, not less. I walked away knowing that I was in the wrong place. I did not belong there any longer. I could not stay.

I desire with everything within me to experience healings and deliverances like the early faith community and apostles experienced! I want to be a part of a community of faith that believes that we will do and participate in even greater miracles than Jesus performed. By his own mouth, Jesus said, *"Amen, amen I tell you. He who puts his trust in Me, the works that I do he will do; and greater than these he will do, because I am going to the Father. And whatever you ask in My name, that I will do, so that the Father may be glorified in the Son. If you ask Me anything in My name, I will do it (John 12:12-14 TLV)."*

"The necessity of prayer is deeply woven into the typology and function of both the ekklesia and the Bride, but it is rather incidental to church, which is why the church rolls without it. Churchianity simply does not see prayer as fundamental to its mission. Perhaps, this is why a true, praying church has been so hard to develop and sustain. Meanwhile, prayer is indispensable to ekklesia. The ekklesia could no longer abandon prayer than a Senator could do his job without voting. Prayer that changes history is fundamental to our DNA." Dean Briggs, Ekklesia Rising, pg. 209-210

What I will proclaim and declare is that since knowing my identity as ekklesia, my prayer life has taken on a new meaning. It has grown exponentially. Since May of 2021, I have participated in an international independent, prayer group called Familia De Oracao via zoom. It began with just two of us and grew to half a dozen people in the first week. We prayed every day for the first 90 days, contending primarily for our adult children—for reconciliation and restoration to Jehovah God first and then to their family. That they would come to their senses and be healed in mind and heart. We have declared healing of father wounds and deliverance from addictions. We have not only contended for our children. Many times, we have lapsed into travail with tears and weeping. Each session lasts for at least an hour, but many times it lasted for one and a half hours, with prayer points and some special requests and testimonials. The rest of the time is spent praying in the spirit. Six different countries with 3 differing languages are represented. It is dynamic!

We are experiencing what Dutch Sheets calls "prophetic action and declaration." He says, "A more complete definition would be: Prophetic action or declaration is something said or done in the natural realm at the direction of God that prepares the way for Him to move in the spiritual realm, which then consequently effects change in the natural realm. How's that for God and man partnering? God says to do or say something. We obey. Our words or actions impact the heavenly realm, which then impacts the natural realm." (pg. 243-244) Intercessory Prayer.

The last week in August, we had 3 people (two in the hospital) with C-19. The two in the hospital were also diagnosed with pneumonia. One did not think he was going to survive. However, they all recovered and walked out of the hospital within a few days. The doctors were amazed. Two of those who were sick were already followers of Jesus and gave Him praise. We are praying for salvation for the other person.

(I want to insert an update on this last gentleman. One of our leaders met him today, September 9th. She stopped by her daughter's place of employment and noticed a group of people around her daughter. When her daughter noticed her, she exclaimed to the gentleman who had been healed, "This is my mum. She has been praying for you." He gave her a big hug and shared his story of how the doctors had given him no hope. At best, they were anticipating they would have to remove one lung and half of the other. Considering the diagnosis, he drafted a will, anticipating he was days or hours from dying.

Plans to meet with him privately and introduce him to the One who healed and restored him are being made. He knows it was nothing that the doctors did because they gave him no hope. He knows it was not another medication because they had nothing to give him. The hand of God spared him in response to our prayers. We must tell him he was given another chance.)

We believe we are praying according to Ephesians 6: 18: *"Pray in the Ruach on every occasion, with all kinds of prayers and requests."* It has only been with the advent of Familia De Oracao Independent International Prayer Group that I have seen vs. 18. This is a command that is attached to the Full Armor of God. This is part of our weaponry. For those who are offended, I challenge you to read the word of God. Acts 1:8 promised "power" for all whom the Ruach came upon. Tongues were a manifestation of the Ruach. Power was the demonstration of His presence. Unless the Holy Spirit has come upon you, you do not have the power to live the Christ-like life, accomplish that which Adonai has tasked you with, or stand against the evil one and his schemes.

Testimonies like this build your faith! We keep putting on the armor of God every day we suit up and do battle in the heavenlies. We believe that this is the authority and power of the Ekklesia and not the church. They are not the same.

I might add that when I moved on from the Community Church, I stayed in touch with my alumni friend. He knew that I had moved on to a Foursquare Church and frequently took liberty in making jabs at my becoming a "holy roller."

128

Having been on both sides of the fence, I want to encourage both sides to repent of their arrogance. The more I study, the more I know about what I don't know, and I know that I don't know. We do great damage to the body of Christ when we get dogmatic about end-time events and setting dates. Things may be playing out differently than the theological system you were taught, and you were adamant everything was going to happen that way. God will act as He will act.

All my life, I was taught pre-tribulation theology. The more I study, the more I become less convinced. Why does the scripture use the term "persevere" (Romans 5: 3; 8:25; 15:5; Ephesians 6:18; 2 Thessalonians 1:4; 1 Timothy 6:11; 2 Timothy 3:10; Titus. 2:2; 2 Peter 1:6; Revelation 1:9; 2:2; 2: 3; 2:19; 13:10; 14:12). If we are gone, what is there to persevere about?

Is pre-tribulation theology mostly a western construct? There are many countries and nations whose czar, king, dictator, or potentate killed his own people en masse. How about Cambodia, Romania, Russia, China, and Germany? Jesus did not come and spare them. Why do we believe we are different?

CLUE: Are these examples from around the world evidence of satanic activity?

The following is an excerpt from my book "Bondslave" regarding 'Mankind: A Common Denominator':

Mankind: A common denominator

All types of slavery are characterized by oppression, persecution, ill-treatment, repression, suppression, subjection, enslavement, tyranny, exploitation, cruelty, ruthlessness, harshness, brutality, injustice, misery, pain, anguish, maltreatment, and subjugation.

The common denominator amongst these various forms of ill-treatment is mankind. All are forms of oppression wielded by man upon man. Some forms are individualized and exercised person to person. Others are institutionalized and wielded by those in control over their subjects, clients, or constituents.

*Some of the most egregious demonstrations of tyranny in history were found in an article titled, "**Here are the 10 Most Cruel and Despotic Leaders of the 20th Century**". To make the list, "there also had to be other less-than-savory attributes exhibited by these leaders. A penchant for violence, murder, genocidal tendencies, and/or other deviances were prerequisites to make this top ten list."*

1. *Idi Amin Dada (In power: 1971-1979) Uganda. He dumped opposition bodies into the Nile River infested with crocodiles.*
2. *Pol Pot (In power: 1975-1979) Cambodia. His methods were starvation, forced labor, torture, and executions of an estimated 1.5 million Cambodians.*
3. *Joseph Stalin (In power: 1929-1953) Russia. An estimated 20 million were executed or perished directly or indirectly under his orders.*
4. *Augusto Pinochet (1973-1990) Chile. He had an estimated 130 thousand arrested and many tortured. Another 3k were executed or removed through forced disappearances.*
5. *Mobutu Sese Seko (1965-1997) Belgian Congo. He later renamed this area, "Zaire". He also gave himself a new name:*

Mobutu Sese Seko Nkuku Ngbondu Wu Za Sanga ("The all-powerful warrior who, because of his endurance and inflexible will to win, goes from conquest to conquest, leaving fire in his wake"). In other words, destruction was his operative. He also acquired an estimated personal fortune of over 5 Billion USD.

6. *Mao Tse Tung (1949-1976) China. Mao was the first chairman of the Community (Communist) party. He instituted many cultural and social reforms, one of which was the infamous "Great Leap Forward" in 1958. The result was one of the worst manmade famines in history where an estimated 40 million people died of starvation.*

7. *Nicolae Ceausescu (1965-1989) Romania. It is estimated that he had as many as 64 thousand people shot and killed. Ceausescu and his wife were executed by firing squad.*

8. *Kim Il Sung (In power 1948-1994) N. Korea. During a three-year period beginning in June 1950, over 2 million Koreans on both sides were killed. N. Korea stayed under Soviet influence while S. Korea stayed under United States stewardship. The war ended in an armistice.*

9. *Mengistu Haile Marram (In power: 1977-1991) Ethiopia. His economic reforms and policies directly contributed to the great famine of the early 1980s, which killed an estimated 1.2 million from famine-related hunger.*

10. *Adolph Hitler (In power: 1933-1945) Germany. Hitler is the most notorious man on this list and probably best known. He came to power leading the Nazi party. "His vehement anti-Semitism would lead to the Holocaust and his desire to conquer Europe would lead to the beginning of World War II. During the war, his Nazi regime would be responsible for an estimated*

19 million civilian and prisoners of war (including those killed in concentration camps)."

[End of excerpt]

This is not what I signed up for!

Do I believe in Jesus' return? Absolutely. When we promote that we have nothing to worry about because we will not be here, the first people to "fall away" will be those that exclaim, "This is not what I signed up for!" They will feel lied to, and I don't blame them.

I can say unequivocally that what God has done in my life over the past 17 years has been transformational. The Holy Spirit has led me on a path that questioned the Church. The questioning and unsettledness began in 2015 and was revealed to me in 2019 prior to our current global event. I hope you will ponder the information I will be sharing with you. I pray that this information will help resolve the yearning in your heart for a new move of God. There is a shaking going on and New Wine is being poured out into New Wineskins.

CHAPTER 12

CHURCH VS EKKLESIA: WHAT IS THE DIFFERENCE? IS THERE A DIFFERENCE?

"Viewed from a certain vantage point, the church has actually done a fantastic job of building what it thinks Jesus committed to, i.e., if we understand Jesus to be building a church, our energies should naturally focus on tending to those who gather regularly to the Lord's house. A church can evangelize, feed the poor, build the family, and run a great Sunday school program (not sure how many churches call it Sunday School these days), but it takes an ekklesia to act with senatorial spiritual authority across their region. That's why the ekklesia is founded on apostles and prophets (Eph. 1:22, 23, 2:20). The mindset of 'sent ones' and 'council visionaries' is different from that of pastors and teachers. Though all are equally important, the chief concern is to rightly prioritize the ekklesial charter."
Dean Briggs, pg. 129 Ekklesia Rising

D ean Briggs continues, "We need an identity transplant." I agree and I shout, Jesus has promised us one through the Spirit. In Romans 12: 1-2, if we will "present our bodies as a living sacrifice — holy and acceptable to God — which is your spiritual service," He promises to do a work of transformation, which will "renew(ing) your mind so that you may discern what the will of God is." If we humble ourselves (repent) and pray and seek His (My) face, He promises to do several things.... including "hear from heaven, forgive our sin, and heal our land (2 Chronicles 7:14)." Are we doing this? Do we feel that we are at fault or complicit in the current situation in our nation? Do you think our land needs healing?

Do you realize that while our nation has been humbled in so many ways and attacked from many directions, the many institutions that have indoctrinated us with the world satanic narratives as well as the church have been brought to their knees and closed?

I find it interesting that the satanic worshipping media, institutions of academia, concert venues, sporting venues, movie theaters, gambling and gaming industries, and churches were all shut down. The purveyors of our thirst for idolatry were all closed. Have you noticed that with the start of the NFL and College football season, their fans are willing to accept the mandate to get their fix? It is escapism in its purest form. We love entertainment, distraction, and seduction. For the genuine lover of Jesus, I encourage you to consider your choice of drug. From coffee to sports, gaming to entertainment, prescription to

Green Crosses, all are hedonistic time wasters. Each of them supports causes that you might not want to be associated with.

I have heard numerous people say, 'I just want things to return to normal (the way things used to be)'. Personally, I hope that is not the case. We in the church have become complacent and deceived, just like the Hebrew children pining for Egypt and the "fish that we used to eat in Egypt for free—the cucumbers, the melons, the leeks, the onions, and the garlic (Num. 11:5)!" They had forgotten the oppression, harsh treatment, and slavery but remembered their indulgences.

My friends, complete the process and come out from the oppression, tyranny, and spiritual slavery of the world system and the church. Jacob 4:4-5 says, *"You adulteresses! Don't you know that friendship with the world is enmity with God? Therefore, whoever wishes to be a friend of the world makes himself an enemy of God." Or do you think that in vain the Scripture says, "He yearns jealously over the spirit which He made to dwell in us?"*

John puts it this way, *"Do not love the world or the things in the world. If anyone loves the world, the love of the Father is not in him. For everything in the world—the desire of the flesh, the desire of the eyes, and the boasting of life is not from the Father but from the world. The world is passing away along with its desire, but the one who does the will of God abides forever."* 1 Jn 2:15-17.

CLUE: What is your identity?

135

Our affections are misplaced! We have fallen in love with the world and its institutions and systems. We love its music, its movies, and its stars. And they are leading us right to the feet of their master. Whether Bob Dylan understood the song he wrote in 1979 or if he lives by it, but the lyrics to "Gotta Serve Somebody" were spot on. "It may be the devil, or it may be the Lord, but we all gotta serve somebody."

Paul says it this way in Romans 6: 17-18 & 22: *"But thanks be to God that though you were slaves of sin, you wholeheartedly obeyed the form of teaching under which you were placed: and after you were set free from sin, you became enslaved to righteousness. But now, having been set free from sin and having become enslaved to God, you have your fruit resulting in holiness. And the outcome is eternal life. For sin's payment is death, but God's gracious gift is eternal life in Messiah Yeshua our Lord."*

Here is a "keyword" chart to assist you in understanding the difference between "Church" and "Ekklesia."

Church	Ekklesia
Institution	Organic
Fixed structure	Mobile, Fluid
Man's design	Jesus' design
Clergy-driven	Laity-driven
Denominational	Unity & Unified vision
Program-driven	People-focused

Impersonal	Highly Personal
Building-based	Home-based
Numbers-driven	Fellowship/Community
Production-focused	Prayer & Worship
Organizational-focused	Biblical Focus
Corporate meetings	Fellowship/Intimacy
General information	Deeper Relationship
Lens of the denomination	Lens of Jesus
Assumed authority	Declared authority
Identity as the Church	Identity as Ekklesia
Acquisition-based	Dispensing
Separation of Clergy/Laity	Everyone Participates
Old Religious form	New Kingdom Movement

I hope that you will also consider "Leaving Church and Becoming Ekklesia" and accept a new lifestyle. This is the title of a book by Tim Kurtz, which is more than a title; it is becoming a move of God.

Embracing Ekklesia and leaving the church has been freeing. For me, what resulted from this shift in identity is an elevated prayer life, new authority, and new discoveries in the Word of God because I am looking with new eyes, a new mind, and a new heart.

My title, Ekklesia Declared, should in no way be construed to be a shot at the born again (of water and spirit), redeemed, set apart, followers of Yeshua, but at the institution that was initiated by men and has created a false construct of being the declaration that Jesus made in Matthew 16:18. It is not true, and we have been misled for over 400 years. It was easier to pass it down from generation to generation as the truth than to question and challenge the heritage of our fathers.

I am not questioning your salvation. I am challenging a false identity that we have assumed and carried far too long. The church has been a yoke upon His followers' necks. A confusing burden falsely placed upon us. Together, let's unite as Ekklesia and become and be who Jesus declared us to be!

CHAPTER 13

WHO SETS THE NARRATIVE?
THE BIBLE SETS THE NARRATIVE!

"Tell me what the world is saying today and I'll tell you what the church will be saying in seven years." Francis Schaeffer

"Thus says Adonai the Maker, Adonai who formed it to make it firm—Adonai is His Name. Call to Me, and I will answer you—I will tell you great and hidden things, which you do not know." Jeremiah 33:2-3

"Have you not known? Have you not heard? Adonai is the eternal God, the Creator of the ends of the earth. He does not grow tired or weary. His understanding is unsearchable." Isaiah 40:28

I just finished reading an article that chronicled a growing portion of Evangelical pastors who are encouraging people to get vaccinated so they can return to worship. There are some noticeably big names who are setting up clinics in church facilities to accommodate the vaccinations of their congregants.

The concern is this: the church is receiving the world narrative and adopting it rather than initiating the narrative. It has been going on for a long time; it's nothing new. We have been deceived and lied to so much that we can no longer determine the truth. The origin points back to the Garden of Eden. The same purveyor of lies, deception, and counterfeit is behind this mass global scheme. The church is not looking beyond what is in front of its face to the grander scheme, which is all linked together.

The deception of this master deceiver is so good, "as to lead astray, if possible, even the chosen (Matthew 24:24)." Who are the chosen? We must imagine they would be our pastors and prophets, our spiritual leaders. God forbid it! They are so caught up and blinded by the system they have helped to create that they cannot see the lie.

Paul tells us the depth of the deception when those entrapped "traded the truth of God for a lie and worshiped and served the creation rather than the Creator (Romans 1:25)."

> *CLUE: When we are caught up in the system, we cannot see the faults, the shortcomings, the deception, or the lies.*

I encourage you to step out of or back from the system and give an honest evaluation. How long has this deception been going on? Since the Garden of Eden. But let us fast-forward to at least the time of Jesus. While he battled with the religious Pharisees, Sadducees, and the Sanhedrin, He also battled a demoniac who lived amongst the tombs (Mark). He cast demons out of Mary Magdalene (Luke 8:2), Jesus confronted demons in the synagogue

(Mark 1:21-28), and He rebuked Satan when Peter spoke (Matthew 16:23). Notice that Jesus told Peter, "You are a stumbling block to Me, for you are not setting your mind on the things of God but the things of men." Is this what we are guilty of?

And He had a battle with Satan after His baptism (Luke 4:1-13). Of emphasis, Jesus was "filled" with and "led" by the Ruach (Holy Spirit). Of interest for our conversation is the closing statement by Luke. *"When the devil had completed every test (may have been more than Luke recorded), he departed from Him until another occasion.*

This indicates that Satan was in no way finished with his testing and scheming. He had only just begun. *To think that Satan is not present today, was not present in the apostle John's Day, is to disregard scripture. It is not even conscionable.*

Satanic activity was present. Even John exposes the liar as "the anti-messiah — the one who denies the Father and the Son (1 John 2:22)."

John makes a startling claim. *CLUE: "This is the spirit of the anti-messiah, which you have heard is coming and now is already in the world (1 John 4:3)."*

John is not talking about our era. He is representing his own time and era. The anti-messiah was currently present and has been in a scheming operation ever since. Are you willing to believe it? Are you willing to receive it? If you think he is only yet to come and not here presently, then we are lacking some common basis. Based on the scriptures I have presented, the spirit of anti-messiah has been present all the time, just not acknowledged or perceived.

If we can accept that Satan's agenda is to steal, slaughter, and destroy, (and I believe create chaos, turmoil, abuse, emotionally cripple, devastate, divide, conqueror, bring pain, sickness, disease, rebellion, war, rape, pillage, plunder, lie, spread untruth, demoralize, frustrate, encourage suicide, abortion, bring destruction upon families) do you need more (John 10:10)?

I just listened to John O'Looney, a U.K. Funeral Director for over 15 years. I encourage you to listen to his story. His position is: "We have been lied to."

CLUE: Fear...the instrument of the evil one!

All the exhortations that Matthew captures in chapter 24 are these: *"Be careful that no one leads you astray (vs. 4). See that you are not alarmed, for this must happen, but it is not yet the end (vs. 6b)."* Fear is the tactic of our collective enemy. Are you caught up in fear? Fear paralyzes and makes one unable to process even simple decisions. Stay in peace, my friend. Peace is the gift of Jesus, and the enemy despises inner tranquility. He promises to "keep you in perfect peace if your mind is focused and stayed on Him (Isaiah 26:3)."

"Then they will hand you over to persecution and will kill you (vs. 9)." We need not be surprised. What was prophesied is being fulfilled.

We must as a kingdom people, as an ekklesia, recapture the narrative and announce, "Thus says Adonai!" We can no longer sit back and accept the narrative of the world, right or left, if it is in opposition to the scriptures. If you can accept my presupposition, that the translation of Matthew 16:18 is Ekklesia and not church, then we have our identity and we have a mandate to be His Ekklesia as a people of His character and as His ruling, governing body. We have responsibilities. Will we now assume them? Will we be "doers" of the word and not "hearers" only?" (Jacob 1:21-25).

> *"So put away all moral filth and excess of evil and receive with humility the implanted word, which is able to save your souls.*
>
> *But be doers of the word and not hearers only, deluding yourselves.*
>
> *For if anyone is a hearer of the word and not a doer, he is like a man who looks at his natural face in a mirror—for once he looks at himself and goes away, and then immediately forgets what sort of person he was.*
>
> *But the one who looks intently into the perfect Torah, the Torah that gives freedom, and continues in it, not becoming a hearer who forgets but a doer who acts—he shall be blessed in what he does."*

We must look in the mirror as Jacob implores. Do we see someone who is ready to answer the call? Or someone who is satisfied sitting in a pew, or a chair, all facing the front? The old is gone and those days we look upon so affectionately are over. The past two years have proven this. There are many who are disenfranchised with the former days, the former religion, the former ways. I hope I can stir you up like Paul was doing to a young Timothy when he said, *"For this reason, I remind you to fan into flame the gift of God, which is in you through the laying on of my hands. For God has not given us a spirit of timidity but of power and love and self-discipline."*

CLUE: The Bible must set the narrative!

The immutability of God is an attribute that "God is unchanging in his character, will, and covenant promises." The Westminster Shorter Catechism says that is "a spirit whose being, wisdom, power, holiness, justice, goodness, and truth are infinite, eternal, and unchangeable." Those things do not change.

> *Ephesians 2:1-2: You were dead in your trespasses and sins. At that time, you walked in the way of this world, in conformity to the ruler of the domain of the air—the ruler of the spirit who is now operating in the sons of disobedience."*

Whatever happened to the days of pastors declaring, "Thus says Adonai?" (Isaiah 43:1, 14; 44:6; 45:11; 48:17; or Nahum 1:12, or Malachi 1:4b, or the many "I AM" statements of Jesus in the book of John). Has God changed His narrative? I understand one of His characteristics is that He is immutable (unchangeable). My bible claims, "Yeshua the Messiah is the same yesterday, today and forever (Hebrews 13:8)." Why have His servants changed the message of the scripture?

From the very beginning of the Bible, God speaks into existence the light, the expanse or sky, the land sprouts grass, the waters swarm with living creatures, the land brings forth living creatures according to their species and then God said, "Let us make man in *Our image*, after *Our likeness*!" Then, "God created humankind in *His image*, in the *image of God* He created him; male and female He created them."

From that point on, Satan has worked and schemed to undermine God's creation by redefining man and attacking our image. Identity and image are powerful and help us to know who we are. The attack on our image and identity is formidable. The progression of attacks on image has elevated in the last 50 years since I was a youth. Awareness of the gay lifestyle was just beginning to awaken. From that point, the advancement of lifestyle promotion on television shows, movies, and ads was noticeable.

The concern is this: today, we are working from the world narrative back to the Bible and trying to Christianize it. We are embracing the narrative that God is love, and that is true. But we are not embracing that God is love and He is several other attributes all at the same time. According to Exodus 34:6-9, He is "compassionate and gracious (God), slow to anger, and abundant in loving-kindness and truth, showing mercy to a thousand generations, forgiving iniquity and transgressions and sin, yet by no means leaving the guilty unpunished, but bringing the iniquity of the fathers upon the children and up to the children's children, to the third and fourth generation."

We are only teaching and preaching an incomplete picture of God. In Proverbs 3:11-12, we hear these words, "My son, never despise Adonai's discipline or dread His correction. For Adonai loves those He reproves, even as a father, the son in whom he delights."

In the New Testament, the Hebrews writer says this, "My Son, do not take lightly the discipline of Adonai or lose heart when you are corrected by Him because Adonai disciplines the one He loves and punishes every son He accepts."

Israel and I have had our share of God's discipline. I hope you have experienced God's discipline for we are told, "If you are without discipline, then you are illegitimate and not sons." That is a daunting statement.

I have found my identity in knowing that I am not the church, which was always confusing. The preaching told us we were the church, but the church was always a location, a building, an inanimate object. We cannot be both. One is living, the other is not. One is breathing, the other is not.

My prayer life and my authority all went to a higher level once I knew my identity. Who did Jesus say I am. It was Jesus who declared to Peter, "Upon this rock I will build My community." My Ekklesia! My ruling, governing body on earth as it is in heaven. Church never told us that we were Ekklesia and those who did only gave us half of the definition. We were told that we were "set apart," but never an authoritative, governing body! Why? They were in control and wanted to keep control just like the king who self-proclaimed his way to becoming the head of the Church of England.

Knowing your identity is everything. I have known several people in my life who were orphaned and spent at least part of their lives in foster care. My hats off to those who provide the valuable service of parenting a child. A teammate on a men's softball team I played on told me his story years ago. He was always searching for his identity. Most orphaned kids do not even have family history for medical purposes let alone who their father is. Many suffer with anger from being abandoned.

He mentioned a statistic to me, which astounded me, so I looked it up to verify. According to www.fostercare2.org, 25% of foster children will be in prison within two years of emancipation and 80% of inmates incarcerated in our prisons have spent time in foster care. I am so glad I grew up in a two-parent family. I am glad I know who my heavenly Father is too!

If you do not believe that identity is important, then why in the past decade have we witnessed a surge in genealogy companies? According to abcnews.go.com in an article by Alan Farnham dated Oct. 24, 2012 and titled, Who's Your Daddy, he states that "Genealogy is becoming a $1.6 billion hobby. FastCompany.com's article titled My Heritage by Neal Ungerleider and dated July 15, 2015 states: "Ancestors Inc.: Inside the Remarkable Rise of the Genealogy Industry boasts 80 million members."

Mankind is looking for their roots, their heritage, and God proclaims that He is our maker, our Creator. Welcome home!

So, how do we reclaim the narrative? Allow me to share first that the enemy of our souls loves to destroy our image, sexuality, and gender. One of the ways he achieves this is by taking hostage that which God has created. For example, let's take a look at the rainbow. I am not aware that any faith organization or church has spoken out about taking something that God created and repurposing it for their narrative—their agenda—turning it upside down and eliminating one color so that it only has 6, which is the number of man. This is an affront to God and should be an affront to us who identify with God.

It has been a slow progression of calling good "evil" and evil "good", which has accelerated over the past two years. Isaiah 5:20 says, *"Oy to those who call evil good and good evil, who present darkness as light and light as darkness, who present bitter as sweet, and sweet as bitter!"*

Paul warns us against digressing into this cauldron of passivity.

He paints a depraved picture of the moral spiral of decline and the consequences of suppressing the truth. God has boundaries and when those boundaries coupled with His lovingkindness are eclipsed, He "gives" people over to their "shameful desires" and "depraved mind" It is a harsh reality, but we must stop preaching anything short of the whole gospel, the full truth of who God is! To do less is not love. It is misleading and false teaching, which secures eternal damnation for all concerned.

I don't care if you are 68 years old like myself or a Timothy in relation to my age! We need Daniels, Shadrachs, and Esthers, Elijahs and Davids to arise today! People who have great faith like that mentioned in Hebrews 11. We serve an Adonai who wants to perform miracles today if only His people will have the faith to call Him into action!

I just completed a study of Genesis 5. I wrote in my journal to our subscriber base, "I hope you read this chapter! I get it, this is a list of dead men who lived long lives."

But how about a few observations. Only a few had their first child before the age of 100. Most lived 800 years after having children. And one never died. The TLV says of this man, *"And Enoch continually walked with God—then he was not there because God took him."* He was different than all the rest of his father's; he "continually," daily, constantly, reverently, humbly, and respectfully "walked with God."

What will be said of you when you pass? Will your life be characterized by others as, "he walked with God?" What a compliment! What would it be like to see your name listed in chapter 11 of Hebrews? Better yet, what will it be like to hear your name announced and written in the Lamb's book of Life?

CHAPTER 14

A BIBLICAL MODEL OF
THE FAITH COMMUNITY

"Without the Holy Spirit, we are nearly defenseless against our own innate tendencies toward self-deception." Francis Frangipane, Holiness, Truth, and the Presence of God. Pg. 19

For false messiahs and false prophets will rise and show great signs and wonders so as to lead astray, if possible, even the chosen." Matthew 24:24

I have been in the Church since I was young. In fact, I cannot remember not being in the Church. There was a time when I was first in college, fresh out of High School in which I was affiliated with a local church that had a traveling musical group. I had experienced an eye-opening summer as an interim Youth Pastor between my senior year in High School and my first year in college, which soured any interest in attending Church. The director was a tenured Family Medical Doctor who embraced my participation in the group. He is a man I admire as he lived his convictions, served as a deacon, and worked tirelessly with the youth of the Church.

My discoveries as an interim Youth Pastor were the revelation that the lives I saw on Sunday did not match what I discovered. I was a student-athlete, playing three sports throughout the school year. My coaches were of the philosophy that you played other sports to keep in shape. So, it was just something you did, and it made you well-rounded as a person. Because of my athletic involvement, I could not participate in the youth program like everyone else. What was happening was that parents would bring Johnny and Susie to Friday night social gatherings and drop them off at the entrance to the education building and they would promptly skip out to go do something else. They were sick of their parents' double standards. Some of the kids, while involved with substance abuse themselves, told on their alcoholic parents, their abusive parents (one dad later ended up serving time in prison), and other lifestyle inconsistencies. I was not prepared for this, and I worked with a senior pastor who, at the time, was mentally retired. All he could speak of was the good old days. He was completely out of touch with this generation.

I later reconciled my feelings about the Church through a musical titled "Come Together" by Jimmy and Carol Owens. If you remember Jamie Owen-Collins, she is their daughter. Come Together was a musical based on the concept "we are all the church" and rather than point fingers at one another, as a body, we needed to be a part of the solution rather than the antagonistic problem. We knew it had weaknesses and imperfections since we were members of the Church. Speaking against the Church was speaking against ourselves.

I bought it and rejoined the body, eventually making a commitment to full-time ministry around 1975. I was licensed shortly thereafter and headed off to Biola University to prepare myself for ministry.

I want to share a reader's digest version of my experience in selecting Biola and the conflict this created with the religious community. At the time of my decision to attend Biola University, the process of discovering Biola was an experience. If you have been in the community of faith for a good portion of your life, you are aware of the terms we use when we are seeking God's direction or "I feel the Holy Spirit is leading." Understand that I was in a Southern Baptist Church at the time and the senior pastor was very open and supportive of my choice.

I didn't even know Biola existed until I attended a Christian Music Conference called Music California in the mid-seventies. I had visited a Southern Baptist College on a vacation in about 1976 and was not impressed by what I found. My High School was bigger than their campus and they only required one Bible Class for basic requirements. I wanted to stay on the west coast. Several well-meaning members of the Southern Baptist Church where I attended as a child and served as the interim Youth Pastor lobbied heavily for Christian Denominational Schools in Texas. I was not interested in the least. I wanted to stay on the west coast.

In 1977, I attended Music California with a High School and College friend. Unbeknownst to me, we had a common High School friend who was attending Biola. My friend informed me that he had spoken with our mutual friend and he had invited us to stop by while in the area. That was fine by me, so we traveled to see our friend on the campus of Biola. I really did not pay attention to the school. If you have seen one campus, you have seen them all. Here is the Gymnasium, here are the dorms, the library, and the classrooms. But it planted a seed and later after returning home, I requested that a school catalog be mailed to me. After reviewing the catalog and praying about it, I made an application, gained acceptance, and received some loan and grant money.

To demonstrate God's providence, the senior pastor I was working with contacted a couple who were members at a former SBC Church he pastored. They took my dad & I in sight unseen and helped to get me acclimated to the area, including an SBC Church, which became our home Church while in Southern California.

We arrived on a Tuesday night at their door and they made us feel right at home. They gave us a lay of the land and informed us that in the area, they were experiencing a "zero vacancy" of available apartments. Well, I felt that God would not bring us this far without providing for us. This was a faith journey, my friends. I was married with a wife and son. I had the backing of my parents and the Church we left. We had a truckload of furniture and a Ford Torino we pulled behind the U-Haul truck. No job, no credit, and no credit cards.

We got up early the next morning to look for an apartment. We stopped at a local grocery store at the bottom of the hill from where they lived and picked up a newspaper. From the store, we went around the block and for several blocks, there was row after row of four-plex units. We drove down one of the streets and I remember my dad yelling stop! I hit the brakes and he said, "Back up." So, I did and there, hidden in the bushes was a "For Rent" sign that had fallen. I hadn't seen it. So, we got out of the car and walked over to this four-plex, walked up the stairs, and fortunately, the owner was inside working on the unit. All the doors were outside leaning against a wall. As we entered the apartment, the first thing we see is a pencil drawing of a woman's face with her hair flowing away from the entry door. There were holes in every door. Quite a bit of repair was needed.

Anyway, if there is a "zero-vacancy" rate and this unit is available, one makes an application. It was more expensive than I was used to paying in Washington State. But we made an application and headed off not at all optimistic at our chances of getting the apartment. Additionally, the landlord informed us that the apartment did not come with a refrigerator as tenants in California were notorious for walking off with refrigerators.

I imagine that we went shopping for refrigerators in the afternoon because I don't recall looking at any other apartments. I know I did not make an application for any others.

Since it was Wednesday, we naturally attended the evening prayer service with our new friends. Our host family introduced us to their Church family and we told our story. They were quite familiar with Biola. Some of the members were students or professors at Biola University or Talbot Seminary. I met a couple of men who were contributors to the newly published New American Standard Bible during my stay. We also requested prayer for our move, an apartment, and a refrigerator.

The next morning, our host's phone rang with the news that one of their friends attending prayer meeting had heard our request for a refrigerator. They had an old refrigerator that they used for soft drinks and they wanted to give it to us. Praise the Lord!

I forgot to mention that the four-plex had a coin-operated washer and dryer. We had a washer & dryer we had brought from Washington State. Ironically, our host's washer and dryer had just gone out, so they purchased them both. It was nothing short of God's providential hand at how He provided, and "yes", we got the apartment. The landlord called a day later offering the apartment to us. I do not recall looking at another apartment. God is good!

A couple of years later, the landlord was working on something and I approached him and said I was curious about something. I said, "I remember walking into the apartment in January of 1978 and we were aware that there was a "zero vacancy" in the area. I had no job, no credit and yet you gave me the apartment. Why?" He looked at me and smiled as he said, "I figured you were a good risk! Your dad was with you."

My dad was with me! In more ways than one! Remember, your heavenly Father is with you too! He promises to be with you!

I will never forget a guest regional SBC Director who attended a Sunday Morning Service a few weeks before I headed to school. He and I struck up a conversation after service and he asked me a question that prompted me to tell him that I was headed to Biola. He looked at me and said, "Son, I predict you will not be a Southern Baptist when you graduate." At the time, I wondered what he meant by that. It did not take me long to figure it out.

We typecast everyone by their titles and associations. God looks on the heart, but man surely looks at the credentials, degrees, and titles. I will still contend; God was in every part of that decision.

I also met professors who were Southern Baptist and taught at Biola either part or full-time. I had an inter-term class with Dr. Gary Chapman, the author of Love Languages. This class was ten years before the Five Love Languages book was published.

The clash I experienced was that Southern Baptist Churches wanted SBC-educated staff who attend SBC schools. Fortunately, I had a couple of men assisting me with getting my name out to Churches, but it was a tough go. I have found the same biases between denominations. As I have progressed in the faith and embraced the giftings and manifestations of the Holy Spirit, the Charismatics did not trust you since you did not grow up Charismatic. They never said it, but you are made to feel like "you are not one of us".

Combine that religious bias with a history of divorce, multiple divorces and the scarlet letter was applied. Could anything good come out of (Nazareth) Washington or Biola? I get it.

The institutional Church protects itself. But what a contrast in traveling to Portugal and having doors opened to you. The very first time I traveled to Portugal, I met an Assembly Pastor. He was Brazilian, so we did not speak each other's language. We required an interpreter. I was introduced to him by Maria. She spotted his son walking on the street. It was a providential meeting. He told me where I was from (and she did not tell him or forewarn him) and we had an immediate spirit connection. Sight unseen, he did not know me, and yet asked me to speak that night at his Church. That was a Friday and I was flying back home the next day. Pastors do not invite strangers to share their pulpit. This would never happen in America. I was invited to preach in three different Churches on my various trips to Portugal and had other opportunities to teach and minister. My trips to Portugal opened my eyes and heart to the nations.

For the church, I did not pass the eye test and even with the works that the Holy Spirit was performing through me, they could not see my heart. That really hurt. How freeing and empowering it has been to discover my identity in Jesus.

I would encourage those who are or have been disenfranchised from the church that God has not forsaken you and is redirecting you back to His original intention, declared by Jesus in Matthew 16:18. I pray for each of us to find each other in a divine display of the supernatural. I am excited to meet you and greet you into a new community as God's Ekklesia. Become today who Jesus declared you to be, "His Ekklesia!"

CHAPTER 15

WHAT DOES EKKLESIA LOOK LIKE? A PROPOSED MODEL.
EKKLESIA D3 (DISCIPLESHIP, DIRECTORY, DISTRIBUTION) CENTER

"They were devoting themselves to the teaching of the emissaries and to fellowship, to breaking bread and to prayers. Fear lay upon every soul, and many wonders and signs were happening through the emissaries. And all who believed were together, having everything in common. They began selling their property and possessions and sharing them with all, including anyone who had need. Day by day, they continued with one mind, spending time at the Temple and breaking bread from house to house. They were sharing meals with gladness and sincerity of heart, praising God and having favor with all the people. And every day, the Lord was adding to their number those being saved." Acts 2: 42 47

J ust like the early community of faith, we face the task of divesting from centuries of established forms of worship centered around a building and the term *"church."* The endearment to the term church is so deeply ingrained in most of us that we are triggered by the mere mention and thought that God could be worshipped and honored without its existence.

Remember that the early Christians came from a heavily steeped religious, legalistic history anchored in the Torah (law). Early Christian Hebrews fought for past traditions of Judaism, especially the law of circumcision. They could not imagine that a Greek follower of Jesus could be a true follower without shedding his own blood (circumcision). They also could not imagine the new faith not revolving around the Temple.

Yet, Jesus told the religious leaders in full view of His disciples what He would do to the Temple.

"In the Temple, He found the merchants selling oxen, sheep, and doves, as well as the moneychangers sitting there. Then He made a whip of cords and drove them all out of the Temple, both the sheep and oxen. He dumped out the coins of the moneychangers and overturned their tables. To those selling doves, He said, "Get these things out of here! Stop making My Father's house a marketplace!" His disciples remembered that it is written, "Zeal for your House will consume Me!" The Judean leaders responded, "What sign do You show us since You are doing these things?" "Destroy this Temple," Yeshua answered them, "and in three days I will raise it up." The Judean leaders then said to Him, "Forty-six years this Temple was being built, and You will raise it up in three days?" But He

was talking about the temple of His body. So after He was raised from the dead, His disciples remembered that He was talking about this. Then they believed the Scripture and the word that Yeshua had spoken." John 2:17-22

CLUE: Jesus' New Community is Centered in People.

What does the phrase "Zeal for your House will consume Me!" mean? Jesus knew what He meant when He said He would "Destroy this Temple," pointing to the physical religious center of Jerusalem. He knew what He meant when He said He would "raise it up in three days." Not only was He resurrected in three days, but the new center of worship and affection was placed in Jesus. Man became the new, living, mobile center of His dwelling. We are His temple!

Paul establishes this concept, this reality in 1 Corinthians 6: 19-20: *"Or don't you know that your body is a temple of the Ruach ha-Kodesh who is in you, whom you have from God, and that you are not your own? For you were bought with a price. Therefore, glorify God in your body."*

Jesus' new kingdom is centered in man, people, and not a building!

Paul provides us with more foundation to this conceptual reality in 1 Corinthians 3:9: "For we are God's co-workers; you are God's field, God's building." Furthermore, the writer of Hebrews states,

"But Messiah, as Son, is over God's house—and we are His house if we hold firm to our boldness and what we are proud to hope."

Can it be any clearer?

All the confusion was created by pastors, teachers, and theologians over the centuries because we have propagated and promoted the concept of church and church as a building. I am not advocating against corporate gatherings. However, the model shows an emphasis on home worship, small gatherings of 2 or 3 people, fellowship from home to home, active participation by everyone attending: *"Instead, be filled with the Ruach, speaking to one another in psalms, hymns, and spiritual songs, singing and making music in your heart to the Lord—always giving thanks for everything to God the Father, in the name of the Lord Yeshua the Messiah (Ephesians 5:18b-20)" and "What is it then, brothers and sisters? Whenever you come together, each one has a psalm, a teaching, a revelation, a tongue, an interpretation. Let all things be done for edification (1 Corinthians 14:26)."*

When I was in the church model, like many, I was guilty of thinking that the ministry is the Pastor's. It is his work and not mine. We also falsely believe that the clergy possesses greater insight into scripture and spiritual things. If we are not careful, our pastor becomes a religious idol. In some cultures, they place the pastor inappropriately high on a pedestal.

You might not be aware, but the position of a senior pastor is filled with narcissists. We have allowed the leadership position in many churches to be filled by men who can be very persuasive, charismatic, great preachers but not pastors, yet they are called a pastor. If a pastor is an under-shepherd, then he needs to be with the flock. Many are not fulfilling the responsibilities of a pastor.

Yeshua told us in an encounter with the woman at the well, *"Woman, believe Me, an hour is coming when you will worship the Father neither on this mountain nor in Jerusalem. You worship what you do not know; we worship what we know, for salvation is from the Jews. But an hour is coming—it is here now—when the true worshipers will worship the Father in spirit and truth, for the Father is seeking such people as His worshipers. God is Spirit, and those who worship Him must worship in spirit and truth." ~John 4: 21-24*

CLUE: *Worship is the Issue, Not Location*

Jesus told her that the location was not important. Man loves to build edifices, which he claims are for God. David did too. When completed, God filled the temple with what is called the Shekinah Glory (2 Chronicles 7). But Solomon had a dream a night later in which God spelled out in specific terms what would happen if Solomon and the nation turned away from God. The Temple did suffer the consequences of his and Israel's actions.

We must worship God in spirit and truth!

CLUE: *We must convert from Acquisition to Distribution*

The money, land, and goods brought and laid at the apostles' feet were not for their personal gain or for a building program and salaries. They were not given so that a church could have millions in a savings account, purchase jewelry, investments, build a portfolio, or place in gold reserves in tunnels beneath their complex.

I do not see this model anywhere in scripture, nor do I see the apostles building themselves palaces or placing a burden upon those they ministered to.

We are told that they had everything in "common." No one was in need of anything as all things were shared in common. You might charge that this sounds like communism.

> *CLUE: No, communism is forced compliance; commonism is a voluntary attitude that all embraced.*

It is a heart issue. Do we own our things or are they owned by God and available for His use? We have a western mentality cloaked in the Torah (the law) of the Hebrews. We feel that we have met the law if we give back to God 10%. I have heard tithing preached for years. What I have come to discover is that God wants our whole heart. When He has our whole heart, He has everything, and we get to manage it. Are you an owner or a manager? When you become a manager, you will discover you have robbed God and that you owe Him everything! It is time we not only divest from the institution of church but also the legalities too.

CLUE: *A change of Attitude comes with your Identity: church or Ekklesia*

For me, the benefits of knowing who I am in Christ, declared by Jesus, have been immense. When I understood the source of the confusion and the source of clarification, the light went on. I had been under the influence of an institution created by man for the express purpose of controlling my relationship with God.

First, with the confusion between church and Ekklesia resolved, I discovered a new authority along with a new identity. Matthew 16: 18 not only became a mandate, but it also became an identity. We were meant to exercise our authority in His kingdom on earth as a ruling, governing body.

Jesus declared His authority to the apostles, disciples, and future disciples (us) in Matthew 28:18-20: **"And *Yeshua* came up to them and spoke to them, saying, *"All authority in heaven and on earth has been given to Me. Go therefore and make disciples of all nations, immersing them in the name of the Father and the Son and the Ruach ha-Kodesh, teaching them to observe all I have commanded you. And remember! I am with you always, even to the end of the age."***

He didn't say "make converts" and He didn't say make denominations and ways to create division. His early community fought off the attacks of the former religious community, Roman oppression, and persecutions, and stayed unified, one in spirit.

165

CLUE: The key difference is that they transitioned from a cultural, religious lifestyle into a spiritual lifestyle striving to establish a new culture, a new community of faith.

They already knew how to walk in a religious, legalistic lifestyle. The transition now was to allow the Holy Spirit to transform them into a new level, a new culture of freedom. They had been enslaved long enough.

When Jesus declares Matthew 16:18-19, *"And I also tell you that you are Peter, and upon this rock I will build My community; and the gates of Sheol will not overpower it. I will give you the keys of the kingdom of heaven. Whatever you forbid on earth will have been forbidden in heaven and what you permit on earth will have been permitted in heaven."*

He is talking about spiritual captives bound by religion, sin, and demonic forces. He is not talking about the external slavery of man, but the internal slavery over man's heart, mind, and soul.

My new identity has changed how I see and interpret scripture. When I discovered the switch of Matthew 16:18 from Ekklesia to church, I began to see other discoveries that brought a whole new interpretation to scripture. I give you a few examples.

In Psalm 118:25, we are prophetically introduced to the Hebrew word, *"Hoshia-na."* By Matthew 21:9 and John 12:13, the crowds are shouting "Hoshia-na to Ben-David!" By insertion of the Hebrew term for our English version, Hosanna, the literal translation, means "save now." What a different picture "save now" brings to the interpretation of this text.

Apostle John gives us an accounting of Yeshua purging the Temple in 2:13-22. How much correlation can we make about how Jesus feels about religious structures, systems, and institutions? I wonder how Jesus feels about what the church in His name has become. As man, have we asked Jesus to bless something that He can no longer bless?

Apostle Luke shares with us a parable (5:36b-39) given by Jesus about *"new wine and new wineskins"*. I have always been taught that this parable is symbolic of new moves of God and the Holy Spirit. I agree with this interpretation. Could it be that God is using our present calamity to purge the church, tear down the religious institution, and establish a new community of faith, His Ekklesia? Luke captured Jesus' final statement: "No man who drinks old wine wants new, because he says, 'The old is fine.'"

My prayer life has also been transformed to a new level. First, Maria and I, prompted by the Holy Spirit, launched an International contending prayer call via zoom named Familia De Oracao (independent of FPM). We started with ourselves and we both invited kedoshim locally and afar to gather with us via zoom.

We discovered that our Western & European friends couldn't be bothered to spend an hour of contending prayer in our native languages mixed with praying in the Spirit. I failed to tell you that this is a 6 a.m. PST call, so for those on the West Coast, it is a different discipline than our friends in Portugal (2 pm). Where we have found the most acceptance and engagement is a group of women in Angola!

As I write this segment, we are around 150 days consecutively (after 90 consecutive days, we no longer met on Sundays), and we average 20 participants during the week. We have a core dozen to fifteen who are with us every day! The sessions are powerful, with testimonies of healings, divine reversals, transformations, and prodigals returning home.

> **CLUE: *Knowing who you are and whose you are is transformative.***

I encourage you to seek God and you will find Him: "When you search for Me with all your heart," (Jeremiah 29:13); to get close to God (if you do, He promises to get close to you, James 4:8); and "Abide in Me (Him), and I will abide in you (John 15:4)." It is a simple formula: "Seek or search, press into or get close to Jesus, and abide in Him!" He promises to "abide" in you when you do your part by "abiding in Him."

CHAPTER 16

PRELIMINARY CLOSING REMARKS

I f we stand back and review the historical record as recorded in the Bible, we hear these words from Adonai, *"Now it came to pass, when Solomon had finished building the House of* Adonai, *the royal palace and all that Solomon was pleased to do, that* Adonai *appeared to Solomon a second time, just as He had appeared to him at Gibeon.* Adonai *said to him: "I have heard your prayer and your petition that you made before Me. I have consecrated this House, which you have built, to put My Name there forever, and My eyes and My heart will be there every day.*

> *"As for you, if you will walk before Me as your father David walked—in integrity of heart and uprightness, doing all I commanded you, keeping My statutes and My ordinances— then I will establish the throne of your kingship over Israel forever, as I promised your father David saying: 'You shall not lack a man on the throne of Israel.'*

> *"But if you or your sons will indeed turn away from following Me—not keeping My mitzvot and My statutes that I set before you—and go and serve other gods and worship them, then I will cut off Israel from the land which I have*

169

given them, and this House which I have consecrated for My Name, I will cast out of My sight. So Israel will become a proverb and a byword among all peoples. This House, now so exalted—everyone passing by it will gasp in shock and hiss, saying: 'Why has ADONAI done thus to this land and to this House?' They will be told: 'Because they forsook ADONAI their God who brought their fathers out of the land of Egypt and embraced other gods, worshipped them and served them. Therefore, ADONAI has brought all this evil on them.'" 1 Kings 9:1-9

Adonai their God told Solomon exactly what He would do if he and the nation "embraced other gods, worshipped them and served them". He would bring evil on them. Adonai was good to His word and He chose Babylon to be His instrument of destruction.

Through priests and prophets like Ezra and Nehemiah, they rebuilt the Temple some 70 years later. But it never reclaimed the earlier glory.

In preparation for Jesus' death, John quotes Yeshua as he speaks about the Temple: *The Jewish feast of Passover was near, so Yeshua went to Jerusalem. In the Temple, He found the merchants selling oxen, sheep, and doves; also the moneychangers sitting there. Then He made a whip of cords and drove them all out of the Temple, both the sheep and oxen. He dumped out the coins of the moneychangers and overturned their tables. To those selling doves, He said, "Get these things out of here! Stop making My Father's house a marketplace!" His disciples remembered that it is written, "Zeal for your House will consume Me!" The Judean leaders responded, "What sign do You show us since You are doing these things?" "Destroy this Temple," Yeshua answered them, "and in three days I will raise it up." The Judean leaders then said to Him, "Forty-six years this Temple was being built, and You will raise it up in three days?" But He was talking about the temple of His body.*

So after He was raised from the dead, His disciples remembered that He was talking about this. Then they believed the Scripture and the word that Yeshua had spoken. John 2:14-22

As Jesus was arrested, his accusers testified, "We heard Him say I will destroy this Temple made with hands and in three days I will build another made without hands (Mark 14:58)."

And Jesus was true to His word. His new Temple dwelt in man. He was now back in a mobile vessel—no longer in a building built by man and made of bricks, stone, wood, and steel. And just like Adam whom He had breathed the breath of life into, He breathed the Holy Spirit, another comforter, into and onto man. And they received power (Acts 1:8).

Paul ministered to the Greeks and Peter the Jewish followers of Yeshua. They met from house to house, growing in strength and numbers. The people were of one mind and one heart. They brought to the apostles the proceeds from the sales of properties and goods, and they *distributed* them so that no one was in need. That which was brought to them was entrusted to them for the needs of others, not for their own personal gain and use. They were not acquisition-motivated, but distribution-driven. We see not one of the apostles using this method for personal gain!

But man over the centuries decided that Adonai needed a house and started building churches, which instituted the law of tithing and religious ceremony and rites and asked God to bless it. Good things have happened in the church despite not being Jesus' instrument of declaration.

> *CLUE: However, do we want to continue to do things our way or Adonai's way? Do we want His blessing, or do we want a king like all the other nations of the world? Will we ever learn that life works much better under His authority and leadership? It works much better when He fights the battles for us.*

Do we really want to feel that we have done our part when we give ten percent? God wants our whole heart and when He has our whole heart, He has all our resources, all our money, time, and talent. We see ourselves as managers, not gatherers. We become managers rather than owners. It is no longer my car, my house, my possessions, but they are on loan from God.

I want to propose a few new concepts. To those who are ministers of the gospel, is retirement a biblical concept or a concept of western civilization that we have swallowed and embraced?

Defeated & Disqualified!

Several years ago, I felt defeated and disqualified. I had survived three divorces and was going through the motions in organized, institutional religion. A good friend of mine showed me Romans 11: 29 and it changed my perspective: *"For the gifts and the calling of God are irrevocable."*

Perhaps, I could regain the anointing I had lost through my sinful lifestyle. I was hopeful, but I knew I had to repent and reconcile with God and my parents and others.

It was a brief time after, during my study of the word, that I came across 2 Timothy 3:1-7: *"But understand this, that in the last days hard times will come—for people will be lovers of self, lovers of money, boastful, arrogant, blasphemers, disobedient to parents, ungrateful, unholy, hardhearted, unforgiving, backbiting, without self-control, brutal, hating what is good, treacherous, reckless, conceited, lovers of pleasure rather than lovers of God, holding to an outward form of godliness but denying its power. Avoid these people! For among these are those who slip into households and deceive weak women weighed down with sins, led away by various desires, always learning yet never able to come to the knowledge of truth."*

The list Paul gives Timothy is a list of the attributes of people's hearts in the last day.

I identified with so many on the list, but the one that humbled me was vs. 5, *"holding to an outward form of godliness but denying its power. Avoid these people!* It was talking about me!

I thought I was godly, but the power was not there. I had been trying to live a godly life in my own power, and I could not achieve that lifestyle. I *repented, reconciled* with God, then my parents and others. Since then, He has *restored our relationship* and *repurposed* my life! I know that I will serve Him the rest of my life. I will live and work for Him the rest of my life. I am His Bondslave.

Another thing I would like is to challenge every baptized follower of Jesus to reconsider how squeezed and indoctrinated we are by the world. It is hard to escape this ritual practice I am about to expose. If you are on social media, Facebook, or LinkedIn, they even reinforce this practice.

Think about how many times our physical birthday is reinforced. We are asked all the time for our physical birthdate for verification. How many times do we share with the world our spiritual birthdate? For most of us, at our baptism only.

If we are truly the new "born again" man we claim, how come we celebrate the "old man" so much? I propose that we institute via the First Place Ministries website a registry for followers of Yeshua, a Spiritual Birthday registry that will send out a notice on that date to remind you and celebrate the New Man with you! Hallelujah!

We quote 2 Corinthians 5:17 frequently. Do we believe it? Not only has He made us a new creation, but...

CLUE: "He has entrusted the message of reconciliation to us. We are therefore ambassadors for Messiah, as though God was making His appeal through us. We beg you on behalf of Messiah to be reconciled with God."

We know the Great Commission, but did you know that He has "entrusted" us with the message of reconciliation? This is another purpose for us. We are to "make disciples" (not converts) and share the message of reconciliation!

Let's get busy, as retirement is only for those who do not understand their purpose in life — to be a bondslave to the King of Kings!

Mankind is looking for their roots, their heritage, and God proclaims that He is our maker, our Creator. Welcome home!

So, how do we reclaim the narrative? Allow me to share first that the enemy of our souls loves to destroy our image, sexuality, and gender. One of the ways he achieves this is by taking hostage that which God has created. For example, let's take a look at the rainbow. I am not aware that any faith organization or church has spoken out about taking something that God created and repurposing it for their narrative, their agenda. Turning it upside down and eliminating one color so that it only has 6, the number of man, is an affront to God and should be an affront to us who identify with God.

It has been a slow progression of calling good "evil" and evil "good", which has accelerated over the past two years. Isaiah 5:20, says, "Oy to those who call evil good and good evil, who present darkness as light and light as darkness, who present bitter as sweet, and sweet as bitter!"

Paul warns us against digressing into this cauldron of passivity.

He paints a depraved picture of the moral spiral of decline and the consequences of suppressing the truth. God has boundaries and when those boundaries coupled with His lovingkindness are eclipsed, He "gives" people over to their "shameful desires" and "depraved mind" It is a harsh reality, but we must stop preaching anything short of the whole gospel, the full truth of who God is! To do less is not love. It is misleading and false teaching, which secures eternal damnation for all concerned.

I hope that we have secured common ground from this journey together through God's word. He has left many "CLUES" for us to find Him, to follow Him (as Ekklesia), and to ultimately be with Him as His bride. The goal of becoming a disciple of Jesus is to become His Ekklesia, His governing, ruling body on earth and to be where HE is in eternity.

Remember that He said, *"Do not let your heart be troubled. Trust in God; trust also in Me. In My Father's house there are many dwelling places. If it were not so, would I have told you that I am going to prepare a place for you? If I go and prepare a place for you, I will come again and take you to Myself, so that where I am you may also be. And you know the way to where I am going." Thomas said to Him, "Master, we don't know where You are going. How can we know the way?" Yeshua said to him, "I am the way, the truth, and the life! No one comes to the Father except through Me. If you have come to know Me, you will know My Father also. From now on, you do know Him and have seen Him."*

> *CLUE: The biggest CLUE I can offer you is this: The board game CLUE was just that—a game. You were playing with someone else's life. The journey God takes us on is for your life, your soul. It all hangs in the balance. Life Eternal is on the line. The battle is between Jesus and Satan. Who will win your allegiance? Whose voice are you listening to?*

"I, John, am the one hearing and seeing these things. And when I heard and saw them, I fell down to worship at the feet of the angel showing me these things. But he tells me, "See that you do not do that! I am a fellow servant with you and your brothers, the prophets, and those keeping the words of this book. <u>Worship God!</u>" Then he tells me, "Do not seal up the words of the prophecy of this book, for the time is near. Let the evildoer still do evil, and the filthy still be filthy, and the righteous still do righteousness, and the holy still be holy. Behold, I am coming soon, and My reward is with Me, to pay back each one according to his deeds. I am the Alpha and the Omega, the First and the Last, the Beginning and the End." *Revelation 22:8-13*

We are His bride; He is our Bridegroom. Let's become who He declared and be ready for His return! Amen.

CHAPTER 17

WHETHER YOU WANT TO ENGAGE OR NOT, THE BATTLE IS ON! THE ENEMY OF OUR SOULS IS AFTER US!

"Our sin is not one of commission but rather omission. Sins of omission are sometimes the most difficult ones to address. To do so requires intentional and relentless self-examination, a commitment to serve those in greatest need, and a keen awareness of the broader world in which God has placed us."
Richard Stearns

So Adonai says, "Since these people draw near with their mouths and honor Me with their lips, yet their hearts are far from Me, and their fear of Me is a mitzvah taught by men."
Isaiah 29:13

Assemble purposefully with an ekklesia mindset. Govern in His name. We need men and women of character, husbands and housewives who will serve quietly and peaceably through the mundane grace of normal life. But when they assemble, they roar. A generation is rising that will discard their preference for lesser pleasures driven by expediency, comfort, and self-gratification. These champions of discipline, wisdom, and selflessness will rally to the mission of Christ because they are enthralled with the revelation of His glory. *They will form loving communities. Of authority and power. And heaven-rattling prayer.*" Dean Briggs pg. 135, Ekklesia Rising.

Life is not returning to the old normal. It is gone just like the Exodus. Do not look back fondly upon the way things used to be. They were not as they appeared. We were deceived. We have no time for nostalgia and reviewing fond memories of the church. For those pastors who have dreams of expanding their building footprint, please reevaluate. A new strategy is needed. The old is being torn down.

I am still on Facebook, and I have a personal account and an account for both The Widows Project and First Place Ministries. Because of my stance on Ekklesia and the church, I am seeking new leadership to assume the vision of The Widows Project. The seven years I spent leading The Widows Project have been phenomenally rewarding. I have learned a lot and enjoyed serving this demographic community.

I am shifting my attention and efforts into the Ekklesia movement. The battle is elevating, and the time is now to engage. While I have focused on hearing from God, I have dropped mainstream media and ended my cable relationship with Comcast Xfinity. I have chosen to follow certain Facebook sources for my information. I am going to share two portions of information from a post by Newspoint of a recent (10/02/21) recorded broadcast of Fox News' Tucker Carlson.

I am aware that there has been so much disinformation (God calls it lying, or false witness) globally today. So, you may totally disqualify what I am about to share without taking a reading of the transcript of a few moments of this broadcast. This is the first time I have listened to anything or anyone from FOX since November 2020.

Here is what was broadcast about the current "Reconciliation Bill" by Tucker Carlson:

> By all accounts, "no one outside of Congress noticed it — a certain provision was there and that's not surprising. The Bill is nearly the biggest (bill) in human history and nearly 2500 pages long. It spent 3.5 trillion dollars. Where does that money come from? Well, it was newly printed by the Federal Reserve for the occasion. The provision in question was hidden on page 168 of that bill. Here's what it says: 'Going forward, the Federal Government will bankrupt any company that refuses to comply with Joe Biden's vaccine mandate. So, do you have an unvaccinated worker in your office? The fine for that will be $700k payable to the U.S. Treasury for each of those workers."

So, pastor, what are the ramifications? Will you have to check everyone at the door and only the vaccinated can worship in person? Will you have to release any staff who is not compliant? Do you really believe a religious exemption will be honored and will satisfy the powers that be? Might you even have to step down from the senior pastoral position?

By now, you might be prompted to understand in the practical, the need and benefit of a change in mindset and lifestyle to the

Ekklesia. If you are going to stand on the sidelines and make a decision to not make a decision, don't bother. God needs people who are willing to face the furnace or the lion's den if that is the cost!

To think that somehow you and your church will avoid bankruptcy and closure is naïve. This is scheming by the master schemer, and it is global. You are being deceived if you think this does not involve you.

I want to close with a quote by Martin Niemöller, a German theologian and Lutheran pastor. He is best known for his opposition to the Nazi regime during the late 1930s and for his widely quoted poem, "First they came...." The poem exists in many versions; the one featured on the United States Holocaust Memorial reads:

> *"First, they came for the socialists and I did not speak out—Because I was not a socialist. Then they came for the trade unionists, and I did not speak out—Because I was not a trade unionist. Then they came for the Jews, and I did not speak out—Because I was not a Jew. Then they came for me—and there was no one left to speak for me."* Wikipedia

CHAPTER 18

PERSONAL MESSAGE

I t will be difficult for your Christian friends once they realize that you have left the "church." They may even be confused. To help them understand, please consider providing them with a copy of this book. They must know that we love them. I hold no animosity to anyone. I know I shared with you wounds from the institution and the people who I have co-ministered and worshipped with over the years. All of us believed in the system and we embraced it and supported it. It was the best we could do with the information we had.

I recently shared this manuscript with a brother, pastor, and friend. He asked me who my target audience was. My response was pastors. I hope they will read and not take offense, but seriously pray and ponder on what they are now aware of. My second target audience is the disenfranchised—those of us who have left the church but have not left our faith. We praise God, we follow Jesus, and invite the Holy Spirit to lead us into all truth. The pandemic era has fortified our faith. I want to reach those who are disappointed, disillusioned, and looking for a viable option to the old system. We are at the same transition, the same crossroads as the early New Testament followers of Jesus. Which will you choose?

We can no longer subject ourselves to the illegitimacy of the church institution model. Man will corrupt everything he institutes and builds. The enemy of our souls will attempt to corrupt and undermine what God has ordained through Jesus, but he will not succeed. He has promised that the very gates of Sheol will not prevail or overpower it!

In his book, Ekklesia Rising, Dean Briggs issues a "summons for legacy-worthy soldier-statesmen to form ranks in the kingdom (pg. 136 Ekklesia Rising)." I agree with Dean, and I issue the same summons combined with an invitation to "become who you were declared to become, Ekklesia!"

The battle has appeared at the doors of our homes. The battle has circumvented the church and come straight for the Ekklesia. We used to think that we could dress in civilian clothing, but I have discovered in the recent past two years that we must dress every day in the *full armor* described in Ephesians 6:10-18. It struck me recently that during times of war and peace, the army still dresses for battle every day. We can do no less. The battle has been brought to us; we had better respond.

We believe that Jesus wants us to "Occupy till I Come." In Luke 19:13b, He says it another way, "Do business until I come back." Either way, He wants us to be actively involved in His kingdom. We will never be a participating, active, governing body with Jesus in His kingdom while being under the control of churches. They do not have the authority they think they have. Be set free in Jesus' name. Amen.

184

I look forward to hearing from you, my friend. Please visit our website and engage with other like-minded followers of Jesus. *Find a group* or *start a group to* intentionally worship and enjoy fellowship with. *Subscribe and receive* our daily *Choose Life Journal* for free in your email box. *Join our International Contending Prayer Group* via zoom.

ADDENDUM #1

THREE SCRIPTURES FOR PERSONAL INVESTIGATION

In working out your salvation, I want to propose three passages of scripture that I do not hear preached upon very often. They are deeply impactful and have been meaningful to me in shaping my approach to lifestyle Christianity. The book of Jacob (James) 1:22 –25 says this: *"But be doers of the word, and not hearers only, deluding yourselves. For if anyone is a hearer of the word and not a doer, he is like a man who looks at his natural face in a mirror — for once he looks at himself and goes away, and then he immediately forgets what sort of person he was. But the one who looks intently into the perfect Torah, the Torah that gives freedom, and continues in it, not becoming a hearer who forgets but a doer who acts — he shall be blessed in what he does."*

I set out to find my "do" about 10 years ago after really seeing and understanding this passage. Finding my "do" or my purpose has been incredibly empowering. It is like finding your calling, along with being called.

I hope, because you've read my book, that you have found your missing identity in Jesus, in being His Ekklesia. If that is the case, I encourage you to find your "do."

I wandered aimlessly for years, attracted to many options, but I could not find and settle on one. And in finding one, I found two. I chose to do one eight years ago, which is sadly drawing to a close. Now I am transitioning to a new one, which is the culmination of an eighteen-year journey.

Now, I understand the dream I was given 18 years ago. Please take the time to allow your choices to be deeply anchored in scripture. Find where God's heart is and then join Him in serving those who hold His heart. I like to say it this way! God loves the world or everybody. He tells us this in John 3:16, a verse we have all memorized. But God has an affinity, a special affection for specific people groups. Who are they? You need to discover this for yourself.

First of all, I would encourage you to look at Isaiah 58. This is a conversation between God and Isaiah. We have all heard a sermon on fasting, but not like this sermon. It will challenge your concept of fasting. We have self-righteously participated in something that remotely resembles a fast in the past, when we come to understand the fast that God wants. The simple question is, do you want to fast God's way or your way? You may end up realizing that what you did in the past did not even qualify!

Secondly, study Matthew 25:31-46:

"Now when the Son of Man comes in His glory, and all the angels with Him, then He will sit on His glorious throne. All the nations will be gathered before Him, and He will separate them from one another, just as the shepherd separates the sheep from the goats. And

He will put the sheep on His right, but the goats on His left. Then the King will say to those on His right, 'Come, you who are blessed by My Father, inherit the kingdom prepared for you from the foundation of the world. For I was hungry and you gave Me something to eat; I was thirsty and you gave Me something to drink; I was a stranger and you invited Me in; I was naked and you clothed Me; I was sick and you visited Me; I was in prison and you came to Me.'"

Then the righteous will answer Him, "Lord, when did we see You hungry and feed You? Or thirsty and give You something to drink? And when did we see You a stranger and invite You in? Or naked and clothe You? When did we see You sick, or in prison, and come to You?"

And answering, the King will say to them, "Amen, I tell you, whatever you did to one of the least of these My brethren, you did it to Me." Then He will also say to those on the left, "Go away from Me, you cursed ones, into the everlasting fire which has been prepared for the devil and his angels. For I was hungry and you gave Me nothing to eat; I was thirsty and you gave Me nothing to drink; I was a stranger and you did not invite Me in; naked and you did not clothe Me; sick and in prison and you did not visit Me."

Then they too will answer, saying, "Lord, when did we see You hungry or thirsty or a stranger or naked or sick or in prison, and did not care for You?" Then He will answer them, saying, "Amen, I tell you, whatever you did not do for one of the least of these, you did not do for Me. These shall go off to everlasting punishment, but the righteous into everlasting life."

"And as much as you've done it to the very least of my brethren, you've done it unto me."

Here's a link to Keith Green's video. Matthew 25 - The Sheep & the Goats – https://youtu.be/Ix8ddosjg-k

The church has been very self-righteous about this passage. The split has been between those who feel that the call to evangelism trumps the call to compassion. So, we have denominations that focus on one side of the equation but dismiss the other side and boast that they are getting it right. My take on this passage is that God knows our hearts and he knows the sheep from the goats. Are you willing to risk only doing part or a portion of that which we have been tasked to do? Because I was raised in the former camp, I have been indoctrinated and I find the compassion part difficult. We are very pharisaical about it, and they were masters in self-righteousness. And here is some free advice: being self-righteous is not a spiritual gift. The question I would ask: Is this a literal judgment? The passage starts out, "Now when the Son of Man comes in His glory, and all the angels with Him, then He will sit on His glorious throne." It is too late at this point to correct your lifestyle. Is the once saved, always saved, which your pastor preached, going to work? Is it going to stand up?

Therefore, I encourage you to get onto our daily Choose Life Journal plan. We post an annual schedule on our website, which you can download and print so you can follow the plan. I have participated in a similar Bible study plan for 17 years. Through this daily discipline, I have discovered that there were things I was told through the teaching and preaching of the word that I do not agree with. The Holy Spirit promises to lead you into all truth (John 16:13). It is an exciting process to join in with the Holy Spirit.

In John's Revelation, Jesus did not tell the churches that they were 'perfect in His eyes.' No! He revealed to them their true conditions; He told them their sins. Without compromise, He placed on them the demand to be overcomers, each in their own unique and difficult circumstance." ~Francis Frangipane

Lastly, at the beginning of Revelation chapters 1-3, John has a visionary download where the Lord speaks to him about the seven "communities" in Asia (remember, I use the TLV exclusively). He is speaking to us. With every community, the Lord has something against them. There are some things we need to address, self-evaluate or upon His return and judgment, He will address these things. Notice the recurrent requests to repent, the recurring mention of the "Synagogue of Satan," the mention of demonic strongholds and 'deep things of Satan,' and everything addressed has urgency because He says, I AM coming soon. There is more satanic, occultic activity around us and in the communities of faith than we realize. Once you embrace the Ekklesia mindset, you will see these scriptures differently.

Considering the current state of our nation and nations of the world, we would do well to study all three passages and heed the prophetic warnings of Revelation. He "knows your deeds." We may think it is our secret, but God is all-knowing and knows the heart of man. He knows yours too.

Your fear will shift to be properly appropriate, from man to God. Matthew 10:28 says, *"And do not fear those who kill the body but cannot kill the soul. Instead, fear the One who is able to destroy both soul and body in Gehenna "*

Get your fear properly placed. Fear Him who has control and presides over eternity!

REFERENCE LINKS FOR YOU

SCRIPTURAL SYSTEM FOR CHRISTIAN STEWARDS –
http://www.wordandwork.org/2018/02/scriptural-system-for-christian-stewards/

As It Was In The Days Of Noah –
http://www.wordandwork.org/2018/02/as-it-was-in-the-days-of-noah/

Children of God: by Birth, or Adoption? –
http://www.wordandwork.org/2018/02/children-of-god-by-birth-or-adoption/

Where Will You Be Then? –
http://www.wordandwork.org/2018/02/where-will-you-be-then/

A New Year's Resolution That Could Make an Eternal Difference –
http://www.wordandwork.org/2018/02/a-new-years-resolution-that-could-make-an-eternal-difference/

Believing In God (Elijah on Mount Carmel) –
http://www.wordandwork.org/2018/02/believing-in-god-elijah-on-mount-carmel/

CLOSING OBSERVATIONS –
http://www.wordandwork.org/2018/02/closing-observations/

FINDING THE LOST SHEEP OF THE HOUSE OF ISRAEL –
http://www.wordandwork.org/2018/02/finding-the-lost-sheep-of-the-house-of-israel/

Balfour Declaration at 100 Years –
http://www.wordandwork.org/2018/02/balfour-declaration-at-100-years/

Moralism is Not the Gospel (But Many Christians Think It Is) –
http://www.wordandwork.org/2018/02/moralism-is-not-the-gospel-but-many-christians-think-it-is/

Paul Harvey's "If I Were the Devil" Transcript from 1965 –
http://www.wordandwork.org/2018/02/paul-harveys-if-i-were-the-devil-transcript-from-1965/

The Forgiveness of God – http://www.wordandwork.org/2018/02/the-forgiveness-of-god/

The Gospel Is For All – http://www.wordandwork.org/2018/02/the-gospel-is-for-all/

The "U" In Jesus – http://www.wordandwork.org/2018/02/the-u-in-jesus/

February 2018 Bible Reading Schedule –
http://www.wordandwork.org/2018/02/february-2018-bible-reading-schedulee/

The Prayer that Turns the World Upside Down –
http://www.wordandwork.org/2018/02/the-prayer-that-turns-the-world-upside-down/

News and Notes – http://www.wordandwork.org/2018/02/news-and-notes-77/

Something Worth Pondering –
http://www.wordandwork.org/2018/02/something-worth-pondering/

* * * * *

In 1965, Paul Harvey broadcasted "If I Were the Devil." It is really amazing to realize how, over 47 years ago, he accurately "prophesied" the future spiritual condition of the United States. Many of his statements were considered ridiculously outlandish at that time in history. Yet, look where we find ourselves today...

Here's another link to that transcript:

https://www.alabamagazette.com/story/2019/07/01/opinion/paul-harveys-if-i-were-the-devil-transcript-1965-even-as-we-see-it-today-2019/1682.html

ADDENDUM #2

WHY I LIKE THE TREE OF LIFE VERSION OF THE BIBLE

Proverbs 3:18: "She (wisdom) is a tree of life to those who embrace her, and blessed will be all who hold firmly to her."

Proverbs 11:30: "The fruit of the righteous is a tree of life, and whoever wins souls is wise."

Proverbs 13:12: "Hope deferred makes the heart sick, but a longing fulfilled is a tree of life."

Proverbs 15:4: "A healing tongue is a tree of life, but a deceitful one crushes the spirit."

Revelation: 2:7b: "To the one who overcomes, I will grant the right to eat from the Tree of Life which is in the Paradise of God."

Revelation: 22:2b: "On either side of the river was a tree of life, bearing twelve kinds of fruit, yielding its fruit each month; and the leaves of the tree were for the healing of the nations."

22:14: *"How fortunate are those who wash their robes, so that they may have the right to the Tree of Life and may enter through the gates into the city."*

195

22:18-19: "I testify to everyone who hears the words of the prophecy of this book. If anyone adds to them, God shall add to him the plagues that are written in this book, and if anyone takes away from the words of the book of this prophecy, God shall take away his share in the Tree of Life and the Holy City, which are written in this book."

I like the Tree of Life Version (TLV) because of the Jewishness of its content. They intentionally set out to break traditional English versions and dared to substitute Hebrew terms for God (ex. Adonai Elyon), Jesus (Yeshua Messiah), Holy Spirit (Ruach), for holy (kadosh) days and festivals (ex. Sukkot) and a host of other traditional Jewish terms like saints or holy ones (kedoshim), peace (shalom), blessings (bracha), and hoshia-na (please save!).

Knowing these terms shines new light on the gospel and new understanding. My last example, "hoshia-na" (our hosanna), came to life this past year in a study of the gospels (Matt. 21:9, Mk 11:9-10, Jn 12:13), where I discovered that the meaning of "hoshia-na" is "save now or please save." The people observing Yeshua's entry into Jerusalem were not only cheering as we preach and portray in our plays and pageants. They were crying out in earnest, "save us now!" We have experienced enough of the oppression at the hands of the Romans soldiers. Perhaps, they had suffered long enough at the hands of the Pharisees, Sadducees, and the Sanhedrin.

Oppression is not an exclusive trait of governments. Matthew, Mark, and Luke each mention the abuse of widows: "They devour widows' houses and make long prayers as a show

(20:47)." Do you think it was legislators that the gospel writers were referring to? I suppose some could be guilty of "long prayers," but he clearly accuses the religious leaders of his time as being the culprits.

Isaiah, on the other hand, also says, *"Oy (Woe) to those enacting unjust decrees and recording corrupt legislation, to deprive the helpless of justice and rob the rights of the poor of My people so that widows may be their spoil and orphans their prey! What will you do on the day of visitation, when desolation comes from afar? To whom will you flee for help? Where will you leave your wealth?*

I had an experience about five years ago that I will never forget. A widow from the East coast contacted me through The Widows Project. She had a home that was in foreclosure, and she had equity. I made several phone calls to pastors in the area, trying to locate legal help. I did not receive one call from anyone willing to help this woman in her area. She had a business too, which was in trouble as well. I believe that with the equity she claimed she had, she could have qualified for a reverse mortgage, saved her home and her equity. She was victimized by predatory lenders. It is not a new concept and has existed both in the governing powers and the religious community in the Bible.

I also like that the translators of the TLV Bible used the term *"communities"* instead of *"church."* They more accurately translated the Greek term "Ekklesia," which means the called out and "a ruling, governing body." This discovery of Matthew 16:18, where Jesus declares to Peter, "Upon this rock I will build My community," is more accurate to the text. The word "church" had not even been invented yet by any language. Its roots come from the German "Kirche."

We fail to realize that the new community of faith was establishing a new identity for the followers of Yeshua. They were breaking away from the religious traditions of the Torah (Law) and its rules like "circumcision." The Jewish side wanted to impose the Laws of its faith upon the Greeks (us). We still experience the same battles today over Charisma and non-Charisma and End Times Theology. How much simpler can we get than to embrace the Apostolic model and the Apostles Creed?

We all want to argue that the Apostolic age is over, but consider how much simpler it is. The problem is man. Rather than embrace a Theocratic model, we like to create titles, denominational names and distinctives, and argue about the non-essential.

Here is how Paul sums it up to a young Timothy. *"Trustworthy is the saying: If we died with Him, we will also live with Him; if we endure, we will also reign with Him; if we deny Him, He will also deny us; if we are faithless, He remains faithful, for He cannot deny Himself. Remind them of these things and solemnly charge them before God not to quarrel about words, which is useless — to the ruin of those who are listening. Make every effort to present yourself before God as tried and true, as an unashamed worker cutting a straight path with the word of truth. But avoid godless chatter, for it will lead to further ungodliness and their words will spread like cancer. Among them are Hymenaeus and Philetus — men who have missed the mark concerning the truth, saying that the resurrection has already taken place. They are overturning the faith of some. Nevertheless, the firm foundation of God stands, having this seal: "The Lord knows those who are His," and "Let everyone who names the name of the Lord keep away from unrighteousness." Now in a great house, there are not only vessels of gold and silver but also of wood and clay – some for honor and some for common use. Therefore, if anyone cleanses himself from these, he will be a vessel for honor – sanctified, useful to the Master, prepared for every good work." 2 Timothy 2:11-21*

Paul also emphasizes the issue in Titus 3: 9: "But avoid foolish controversies and genealogies and strife and disputes about Torah, for they are unprofitable and useless."

Is it really worth it? Does it accomplish God's work? Or does it just implicate us all? I am guilty if I perpetuate the non-truth of most translations.

I also like the TLV because it more accurately conveys the subtle distinctive difference in the Greek word, "Doulos" meaning either slave or servant. Most translations, including King James, use the word "servant." The TLV correctly uses the word "slave." I wrote on this topic in my last book, BONDSLAVE: THE INCONVENIENT TRUTH ABOUT YOUR IDENTITY IN CHRIST.

My conviction is that Paul was talking about being a "slave" of Yeshua when he lists all the suffering he has experienced to the Corinthians. Servants do not endure prison, beatings, forty lashes minus one five times, stoned, three shipwrecks, danger from floods and robbers, danger at sea, sleepless nights, hunger, and thirst, cold and exposure. Do servants endure this type of treatment? I do not believe so. After all, the Lord prophesied that he was going to show Paul how much he must "suffer for My name's sake (Acts 9:16)."

EKKLESIA DECLARED!

In Romans 6, Paul is abundantly clear that he is talking about spiritual slavery. We once were "slaves to sin," but now you are "slaves to righteousness." How many pastors have told you this? Few, because it is not politically correct to talk about slavery in any form today. It may not be popular, but it is the truth. We are slaves to that which we obey. Paul encourages us to be "set free from sin and having become enslaved to God, you have your fruit resulting in holiness. And the outcome is eternal life (vs. 22)." I encourage you to become and identify as a bondslave of Yeshua Messiah!

Just as an aside, I believe that King James (I do not respect him any more than I respect Satan) also had the Greek term "Doulos" translated as servant for this reason. What was the primary financial mechanism in his country? Slavery. He did not want to disparage that which he was involved in.

Man oppresses and Yeshua frees. We have seen it throughout history. Yeshua understands intimately man's heart. We like to say they are good people. Adonai says the "heart is deceitful above all things, and incurable (it is redeemable though) — who can know it? I, Adonai, search the heart; I try the mind, to give every man according to his ways, according to his deeds (Jeremiah 17:9-10)."

I should add that I do not hold King James as singularly responsible. There are 47 theologians who are culpable. I am personally concerned for their souls. They knowingly bowed to the king's wishes and were disobedient to the King of Kings. There are consequences to their actions explained in Revelation

22: 18b-19: "I testify to everyone who hears the words of the prophecy of this book. If anyone adds to them, God shall add to him the plagues that are written in this book; and if anyone takes away from the words of the book of this prophecy, God shall take away his share in the Tree of Life and the Holy City, which are written in this book."

Let us *not* continue to perpetuate a lie.

I want to quote Dr. Jeffrey L. Seif, Tanakh Project Manager and Vice President, *"We believe that reckonings of Hebrew, Aramaic, and Greek manuscripts have all too often been tendered by churchmen with little to no intellectual interest in the Jewish experience, no emotional connection to the Jewish people, and no real personal support for the Jewish homeland – Israel. The upshot of the disregard, be it intentional or accidental, is that biblical books that were written to Jews, for Jews, and about Jews lose a critical element – their actual Jewish essence. Readers wanting to come to terms with the Bible's messages, messengers, and recipients are thus all too easily directed away from the main Author's storylines and intents. Jewish displacement and replacement motifs come through in ways that are subtle and in ways that are not so subtle. Either way, and the translator's intentions aside, God's will and ways can be obscured through their jaded bias. The result is that anti-biblical prejudice germinates, the anti-biblical soul sickness inadvertently passes on to the next generation of Bible readers, and the world all too easily suffers the loss of a vision of What God is up to in HIs Word and in His world."* (pg. X, TLV Bible)

He is absolutely correct. This has gone on for generations, being handed down as gospel and the only true authority. I unapologetically say that I can no longer support the institution of church. I am cautious about the KJV of the Bible. The king had an objective and he succeeded in controlling his kingdom. That control has reached across the seas and subjected many to a man-made, religious culture — one in which he tried to usurp the true Head of his bride, Yeshua. He is like his father who also tried to usurp the God (Elohim), the true Sovereign of heaven and earth. I declare that there is only one true Sovereign, and it is not King James.

ADDENDUM #3

ADAPTED GUIDELINES

The following guidelines are adapted from the book "Leaving Church Becoming Ekklesia" by Tim Kurtz [used with the express permission granted by Tim Kurtz] copyright 2017, Kingdom Word Publications.

1. **Intentionally Gather on a regular and frequent basis**: Most followers of Jesus have been programmed to 'go to church' every Sunday morning. You have a new flexibility. Most New Testament followers were meeting daily, breaking bread, and studying the word (Acts 2:42-47 & Acts 17:11). They lived in close community, so gathering was spontaneous and intimate. If you live in a small town or community, or live next door to an extended family, you may be able to commune almost daily. Intentionally meet when most convenient.

2. **The Purpose of Gathering Supersedes the location:** The primary location is the home. This is no less spiritual because you gather in a home rather than a dedicated building. Remember that you are allowing the Holy Spirit to build a "family," not an organization (John 4:21-24). Your primary purpose is to understand as much as you

can about the ekklesia and to get to know each other. This would be apostolic doctrine and fellowship (Acts 2:42). Share and grow together.

3. **You are Gathering to 'Live Life' Among other Believers:** Those who gather with you are your family. You are not 'members' of an organization—you are a living organic body of believers. We recommend that you gather at least two or three times every month. However, your relationships should extend beyond the times you gather (1 Corinthians 12:24b-26). Make a strong and intentional effort to be involved in the lives of your sisters and brothers throughout the week. The key point is, don't simply settle for seeing and ministering to each other when you meet as a group.

4. **Commit to Building Trust Among Each Other:** The more you gather, the more you will learn about each other.

    A. You build trust with each other as you keep each other's personal matters confidential and pray for each other's needs.

    B. You build trust by being open and honest with one another in love (Romans 12: 3-21; James 5:16).

    C. You build trust by committing to work misunderstandings and disagreements. If they occur, don't let division be among you.

    D. Don't allow doctrinal differences to bring division. Find ways to equitably search out the Word of God rather than allow doctrine to divide you.

E. You build trust by refusing to allow anyone outside of your gatherings to disparage or criticize anyone in your fellowship.

5. **In Every Gathering, Be Intentional about Edifying, Exhorting, and Comforting One Another:** Prophecy edifies the Ekklesia (1 Corinthians 14: 3 & 2 Corinthians 1: 3-7). Every time you gather with your brothers and sisters, seek ways to build life in each other. Always seek ways to encourage each other. Consider every person as someone valuable to the Kingdom of God. Each of us has varying gifts. Confirm and affirm those gifts in each other. I have met brothers and sisters who have the skills and heart to run for school boards or city office. We need ekklesia in every facet of local, regional, state, and national office. We need Ekklesia in our medical, educational, legal, and financial institutions. Encourage those who would stand up for Christian values in decision-making areas of life.

6. **Every Gathering is not the same – Follow the Holy Spirit's Lead:** Do not get locked into a rigid structure or routine. The Holy Spirit leads your gathering. One week you may find yourself discussing scripture. Another week, maybe all praise, prayer, and worship. Other times, maybe all fellowship (1 Corinthians 14:26-32).

7. **Do not look for one person to 'preach' or 'teach' during your regular gathering:** Attend each gathering ready to share what God has shown you. If you are not engaging in a daily Berean Lifestyle (Acts 17:10-11) of time in the Word, please consider plugging into a daily system like

the Choose Life Journal. It will be difficult for you to participate in an ekklesia group if you are not engaged with the lifestyle. Daily time in the Word and Prayer keeps you in close relationship with God and man. If your vertical relationship is suffering, it is most likely that your horizontal relationships are also struggling.

8. **Do Not put time limits on your gatherings:** However, be considerate of your host. If they are someone who must get up early for work, be respectful. If the Spirit is flowing, please flow with Him.

9. **Share a Fellowship meal at every gathering:** You may begin a gathering with a meal, or you may close a gathering with snacks. Some have a policy that the food has to be available at any time, even during the gathering. Again, be respectful of the host. If they want to keep the food in a certain area, honor their feelings. You are a guest in their home. If they take their shoes off upon entering their home, do as they do. If they don't eat in the living room or family room, please keep the food in the eating area. And if possible, help clean up!

10. **Share the Lord's Table often:** Some partake of the Lord's meal in every gathering. Establish your ekklesia's policy to fit the personality of your group. But we encourage you to observe often. Many of you have been taught that Communion, the Eucharist, or the Lord's Table can only be administered by an 'ordained clergy'. To limit this to 'clergy' cannot be substantiated by scripture. This is an ordinance for all believers. (For more information, you

may consider getting a copy of The Lord's Table, available from www.TheEkklesiaCenter.org). Sharing Communion is one of the greatest and blessed things you can observe at your gatherings.

11. **Utilize The Resources Available:** Clearly, this is new to many. Therefore, we have provided a list of resources that may be helpful. Take advantage of them. Prayerfully, we are seeking innovative ways to help minister to people around the world. Zoom has become an accepted method of meeting like-minded ekklesia, holding prayer meetings, training, teaching, and networking. First Place Ministries has resources for disciplining in bible study and prayer. https://www.firstplaceministries.com/.

12. **Prayer:** *Pray at all times in the Spirit* (Col. 4:2 & Eph. 6:18). This book, or any other book you read, cannot take the place of the Word of God, or the work of the Holy Spirit in you. Seek the Lord every step of the way. In your gatherings, pray with each other and for each other. Pray in agreement based on Matthew 18:19-20, *"Again I say to you, that if two of you agree on earth about anything they may ask, it shall be done for them by My Father in heaven. For where two or three are gathered together in My name, there I am in their midst."*

Pray that the Lord will reveal His ekklesia in your area and ultimately on earth. Pray for lost souls. And I humbly ask that you pray for this ministry work so that we will accomplish all that the Lord has called us to do.

ABOUT THE AUTHOR

Rolland is the Founder and President of First Place Ministries. He is also the Founder and past President of The Widows Project.

This is Rolland's third book, following The Widows Project: Serving the Widowed With The Father's Heart; and BondSlave: The Inconvenient Truth About Your Identity In Christ.

He is an Alumnus of BIOLA University.

His two (2) life verses are Acts 17:28 (TLV) "For in Him we live and move and have our being" and Colossians 1:18b (TLV) "so that He might come to have first place in all things."

Rolland has a son Chris married to Cindy (2 daughters Chloe & Brenna); 2 daughters, Jennifer married to Nick (son Carter & daughter Kaylee) and Bethany (daughter Brooke). Rolland's parents celebrated their 69th wedding anniversary in June 2021.

ABOUT FIRST PLACE MINISTRIES

First Place Ministries (FPM) is home to the Ekklesia Center D3 Hub. Register your Ekklesia Home group for free or find a group to fellowship with like-minded worshipers.

FPM was founded with the vision to help Jesus followers establish a Berean Lifestyle of daily time in the Bible. Utilizing an inductive study method has emerged the Choose Life Journal system based on the acronym PRAAYER (Prayer, Reading, Attention, Action, Yielding, Engaging, Relationship). The plan gives the reader the flexibility to accomplish the complete study of the Bible in 1-3 years. You decide. Subscribe for free at www.firstplaceministries.com.

PLEASE RATE MY BOOK

I would be honored if you would take a few moments to rate our book on Amazon.com.

A five-star rating and a short comment ("Very informative!" or "I know at least 3 people who could benefit from this book!") would be much appreciated. I welcome longer, positive comments as well.

If you feel like this book should be rated at three stars or fewer, please hold off posting your comments on Amazon.

Instead, please send your feedback directly to me, so that I could use it to improve the next edition. I'm committed to providing the best value to our readers, and your thoughts can make that possible.

You can reach me at Rolland@firstplaceministries.com.

Thank you very much,

Rolland Wright
President & Founder, First Place Ministries
www.firstplaceministries.com

Made in the USA
Middletown, DE
21 February 2022